# SHAKESPEARE'S
# *The Merchant of Venice*

### Alan Ablewhite

**GREENWICH EXCHANGE
LONDON**

**Greenwich Exchange, London**

Shakespeare's *The Merchant of Venice*
© Alan Ablewhite 2007

First published in Great Britain in 2007
All rights reserved

This book is sold subject to the conditions that it shall not, by way of trade or otherwise, be lent, resold, hired out, or otherwise circulated without the publisher's prior consent in any form of binding or cover other than that in which it is published and without a similar condition including this condition being imposed on the subsequent publisher.

Printed and bound by Q3 Digital/Litho, Loughborough
Tel: 01509 213456
Typesetting and layout by Albion Associates, London
Tel: 020 8852 4646
Cover design by December Publications, Belfast
Tel: 028 90352059

Cover: Colin Willoughby: Arena Images.

Greenwich Exchange Website: www.greenex.co.uk

Cataloguing in Publication Data is available from the British Library

ISBN-13: 978-1-871551-96-9
ISBN-10: 1-871551-96-X

*With love to my wife Gill, who is a constant support and inspiration, and to Brian, Neil and John for bringing the characters to life.*

# Contents

| | | |
|---|---|---|
| Introduction | | vii |
| 1 | Antonio | 1 |
| 2 | Lorenzo and Bassanio | 9 |
| 3 | Shylock | 22 |
| 4 | Portia | 32 |
| 5 | Gratiano and Nerissa | 39 |
| 6 | Send in the clowns | 46 |
| 7 | The play on stage | 50 |
| Bibliography | | 57 |

# Introduction

*The Merchant of Venice* is one of Shakespeare's relatively early works. The play is generally thought to date from 1596 to 1598. Certainly, in 1596, the Spanish ship the *St Andrew* (sic, but actually the *San Andrès*) was captured at Cadiz. This is believed to be the ship referred to by Salerio:

> But I should think of shallow and of flats
> And see my wealthy Andrew docked in sand,
> Veiling her high-top lower than her ribs
> To kiss her burial.
> (Act I, scene 1, 26-9)

In 1598 the *Stationers' Register* mentions "a booke of the *Merchaunt of Venyce*, or otherwise called *The Jewe of Venyce*". The first quarto (published in 1600) says on the title-page that *The Merchant of Venice* had been "diuers times acted by the Lord Chamberlaine his seruants". Francis Meres names the play in Palladis Tamia, published in 1598, so it must have been known to the public by then. The play may well have been first performed by the Lord Chamberlain's Men but the first recorded performance is 10th February 1605, Shrove Tuesday, when the King's Men played it before King James I, who liked it well enough to command a second performance the following Tuesday.

It thus comes after *Loves Labours Lost*, *Romeo and Juliet*, *Richard II*, *A Midsummer Night's Dream* and *King John*, and just before *Henry IV* Parts I and II and *Much Ado About Nothing*. In other words it lies right in the middle of Shakespeare's first major creative phase during the last years of the reign of Elizabeth I.

*The Merchant of Venice* is listed as a comedy. If comedy means that it is funny and there are likeable heroes and heroines and a happy ending, then I wonder whether the play (or any of several others written by Shakespeare) is truly a comedy. Of the three intertwined stories, one has a tragic ending, while the other two end more or less happily, although you need to be an optimist to think that the characters will be happy ever after.

The first strand involves Bassanio, who is deeply loved by Antonio, the merchant of the title, and who frequently relies on that love to receive large sums of money which he then loses on risky ventures. On a previous visit to Belmont he has seen the rich heiress, Portia, and realised that she has fallen in love with him. If he could marry her, he would be able to repay his debts to Antonio – but first he would need to borrow yet more, to finance the expedition. So Antonio risks his life to borrow the money from the Jew, Shylock, whom he, along with many of the other Venetians, deeply despises as an alien to be spat upon.

The second strand is the story of Shylock himself. He is an alien in a foreign land who has become successful but who risks his wealth, his place among his friends, and even his life, for revenge. He hates the Christian Antonio because he forces down the interest rate. In the vain hope that it might succeed, he proposes a deal which would kill Antonio. When his daughter Jessica elopes with a headstrong young Christian, taking his jewels with her, and Antonio's ships are wrecked, he takes his revenge, but to his own downfall. Is the play anti-Semitic? Certainly many of the characters are, including the hero and heroine, the Duke and Antonio. But Shakespeare gives Shylock the chance to put his side of the argument and it is impossible not to feel for him in his fall. He is, as I hope to demonstrate, a genuinely tragic figure.

The third strand is the only romantic love story: that of Lorenzo and Jessica. Here love crosses racial and religious boundaries, as the Jewish Jessica risks her father's love for ever by running away with the Christian Lorenzo. We are led to believe that they will be happy, but their love leads in part to Shylock's downfall. With the echoes of *Romeo and Juliet*, written only three or four years earlier, you are left wondering whether they will.

At the resolution of the play, Shylock is destroyed; Antonio is rich, but may well have lost his love as Bassanio and Portia are married; and Lorenzo has his Jessica. But one cannot help feeling that it is the lusty and uncomplicated union of the worldly-wise observer Gratiano and the clear-headed Nerissa which is more likely to be happy than either the romantic attachment of Lorenzo and Jessica or the primarily financial marriage contracted by Bassanio.

It is the purpose of this book to provide some arguments and evidence to help you make up your own mind. Since a play only exists in its characters, I have adopted the device of providing these arguments by analysing the main characters in turn, starting with the Merchant of Venice himself.

# 1

# Antonio

The first thing that strikes one about *The Merchant of Venice* is the title. Why is it so called when the 'hero' is Bassanio and the tragic figure would seem to be Shylock? Is the play about Antonio? Perhaps it is, but only in the same way that *Julius Caesar* (which is, at least in performance, really the tragedy of Brutus) is about Caesar? Perhaps Antonio, like Caesar, is a catalyst by which the actions of others are caused to bring their own existential personal tragedies or triumphs to a resolution. Too often in production, Antonio can be a rather faceless, uninteresting role. Certainly to most people 'The Merchant' does not immediately conjure up Antonio, but rather Shylock. This was clearly always so, as can be seen from the alternative title in *The Stationers' Register, The Jewe of Venyce*.

And yet Antonio is the centre of one of the main intertwining stories in the play, namely the love of an older man for a younger and the sacrifice he is prepared to make for him. This chapter will explore the relationships of Antonio with Bassanio and with Shylock and the way in which they shape the narrative and lead to the outcome.

Antonio loves Bassanio. This is clearly stated:

> You know me well, and herein spend but time
> To wind about my love with circumstance;
> And out of doubt you do me now more wrong
> In making question of my uttermost
> Than if you had made waste of all I have.
> Then do but say to me what I should do
> That in your knowledge may by me be done,
> And I am prest unto it. Therefore, speak.
> 
> (Act I, scene 1, 153-60)

> Say how I loved you, speak me fair in death,
> And when the tale is told, bid her be judge
> Whether Bassanio had not once a love.
>
> (Act IV, scene 1, 272-4)

Throughout the play there is an ambivalence about what kind of love it is. At the start of the play, Antonio is teased by his friends when Bassanio appears:

> ANTONIO
> ... my merchandise makes me not sad.
> SOLANIO
> Why, then you are in love.
> ANTONIO
> Fie, fie!
> SOLANIO
> Not in love neither? Then let us say you are sad
> Because you are not merry; and 'twere as easy
> For you to laugh and leap, and say you are merry
> Because you are not sad.
>
> (Act I, scene 1, 45-50)

From this it is clear that Solanio certainly suspects a homoerotic relationship. The term 'in love' is not used of non-sexual love. Indeed, Solanio and Salerio are frequently played as camp gay men. It is difficult to take a view on this from the 21st century. In Elizabethan society, a kind of bisexual camaraderie was apparently the norm as can be seen from the sonnets written to a young man, particularly Sonnet 20:

> A woman's face, with Nature's own hand painted,
> Hast thou, the master-mistress of my passion;
> A woman's gentle heart, but not acquainted
> With shifting change, as is false women's fashion;
> An eye more bright than theirs, less false in rolling,
> Gilding the object whereupon it gazeth;
> A man in hue all hues in his controlling,
> Which steals men's eyes, and women's souls amazeth.
> And for a woman wert thou first created;
> Till Nature, as she wrought thee, fell a-doting,

> And by addition me of thee defeated,
> By adding one thing to my purpose nothing.
>> But since she pricked thee out for women's pleasure,
>> Mine be thy love, and thy love's use their treasure.

Or, to paraphrase the last couplet: Since nature gave you a penis, which will pleasure women, then pleasure them (if you must) but *love* me.

Other examples can be found in the friendship of Antonio for Sebastian in *Twelfth Night* and, arguably, of Coriolanus for Aufidius. The best summation of this kind of relationship was made by Oscar Wilde at his trial in 1895:

> 'The love that dares not speak its name' in this century is such a great affection of an elder for a younger man as there was between David and Jonathan, such as Plato made the very basis of his philosophy, and such as you find in the sonnets of Michelangelo and Shakespeare. It is that deep spiritual affection that is as pure as it is perfect. It dictates and pervades great works of art, like those of Shakespeare and Michelangelo, and those two letters of mine, such as they are. It is in this century misunderstood, so much misunderstood that it may be described as 'the love that dares not speak its name' and on that account of it I am placed where I am now. It is beautiful, it is fine, it is the noblest form of affection. There is nothing unnatural about it. It is intellectual, and it repeatedly exists between an older and a younger man, when the older man has intellect, and the younger man has all the joy, hope and glamour of life before him. That it should be so, the world does not understand. The world mocks at it, and sometimes puts one in the pillory for it.

Is the relationship between Antonio and Bassanio such a love? The alternative view is that Antonio is a bachelor who found the son he never had and cared for him in a parental way. I don't think this really agrees with Solanio's teasing and with the nature of the intended sacrifice:

> Repent but you that you shall lose your friend,
> And he repents not that he pays your debt,

> For if the Jew do cut but deep enough,
> I'll pay it instantly with all my heart.
>
> (Act IV, scene 1, 275-8)

I feel that there is definitely something much more intense than a father/son relationship here.

In recent productions, Antonio has been played in the way I suggest: notably by Jeremy Irons in the 2005 film by Michael Radford. Apparently, Irons was not Radford's first choice for the part. He originally tried to cast Ian McKellan who might have brought an even more homoerotic reading to the part than Jeremy Irons did. The relationship was underlined in that film by a rather clumsy location of one scene actually in Antonio's bedroom, as if Bassanio was quite at home there.

The actor, Sir Ian McKellen, a key figure in the gay rights community, says he is convinced Shakespeare was homosexual because of his depiction of gay relationships. McKellen says, "Did he sleep with another man? I would say yes. An examination of his plays makes it clear that Shakespeare had a close understanding of gay relationships. Look to where it matters: his work, where Shakespeare certainly writes about gay people. One part which I want to play is Antonio in *The Merchant of Venice*. His first line is: 'In sooth, I know not why I am so sad'. The audience knows that it's because his boyfriend has come to him to borrow money to get married."

To McKellen the play is built around the love triangle between an older man, a younger man and a woman. "*The Merchant of Venice* centres on how the world treats gay people as well as Jews." Other commentators disagree. And indeed it is slightly difficult to accept the subsequent relationship of Bassanio with Portia if Bassanio is actually gay himself. Of course, he might be bisexual or just a heterosexual totally at ease with being loved by a gay man – especially if money flows from it!

An interesting modern comparison might be the relationship between the great film director Lindsay Anderson and the actor Malcolm McDowell, with whom he worked on a number of films. McDowell says:

> Lindsay was honestly my best friend who wasn't a contemporary. I never looked at him as a mentor, and I don't really like the term, but I suppose he was. I knew that if there was ever any apologising to be done, it would probably have to be from me. That was the price of the relationship.
>
> He was gay, but he was a celibate homosexual. All the people that he loved were unattainable because they were heterosexual. I didn't really know that he was gay, and I wasn't going to ask him because it wasn't my business. He never, in any way, made a pass at me, although he took an enormous interest in me as a person, which I suppose had homosexual overtones to it. But sex was never an issue.
>
> When he died, well what can you say? It didn't sink in for a while. And then you realise there are no more phone calls. But I never crossed his number out of my phone book. It's still there now.

When I directed the play recently for Brentwood Shakespeare Company, I gave the actor playing Bassanio the whole of the *Guardian* article from which that passage is quoted. I didn't give it to the actor playing Antonio. The result was a wonderfully emotionally understated but deep relationship between the two characters, each approaching the other in a different way.

In the 1997 version by the Royal Shakespeare Company directed by (the gay) Gregory Doran the relationship was not over-signalled. Jeremy Kingston in *The Times* wrote:

> The homoerotic bond between Bassanio and Antonio is only half-heartedly suggested when Julian Curry shrinks into himself at the young man's pressing touch.

Reviewing a later RSC production by Lindsay Ingram, Charles Spencer in the *Daily Telegraph* wrote of Ian Gelder's genuinely touching performance as Antonio, whom he presents as a lonely, dignified homosexual, hopelessly besotted with Bassanio.

An interesting slant is put on this interpretation by the ring sub-plot in Act V. Note that Bassanio receives back the ring from Portia via Antonio, which does suggest a certain knowingness on the part of all three characters as to the true nature of the unstated relationships. There is no way of being certain about any of this – which is one of the great joys of Shakespearean analysis. In the end it is down to what you personally believe. I will revisit this relationship when discussing Bassanio later.

What of Antonio as a businessman and citizen? He seems to have no close friends – Solanio and Salerio are clearly mere acquaintances (or possibly friends in a gay coterie?). Indeed, when Bassanio appears, they tend to makes their excuses and depart rapidly.

He ventures capital on importing goods from all over the known world:

> My ventures are not in one bottom trusted,
> Nor to one place; nor is my whole estate
> Upon the fortune of this present year.
> 
> (Act I, scene 1, 42-4)

and:

> He hath an argosy bound to Tripolis, another to the Indies; I understand, moreover, upon the Rialto, he hath a third at Mexico, a fourth for England, and other ventures he hath squandered abroad.
> 
> (Act I, scene 3, 17-21)

He is recognised as being a good investment by the financial markets:

> Thou know'st that all my fortunes are at sea,
> Neither have I money, nor commodity
> To raise a present sum. Therefore go forth;
> Try what my credit can in Venice do,
> That shall be racked even to the uttermost
> To furnish thee to Belmont, to fair Portia.
> Go presently inquire, and so will I,
> Where money is; and I no question make
> To have it of my trust or for my sake.
> 
> (Act I, scene 1, 177-85)

And, like all of commercial Venice, he traded with, but despised the Jews:

> You call me misbeliever, cut-throat dog,
> And spit upon my Jewish gaberdine,
> And all for use of that which is mine own.
>
> (Act I, scene 3, 108-10)

about which he is frankly unapologetic:

> I am as like to call thee so again,
> To spit on thee again, to spurn thee too.
>
> (Act I, scene 3, 127-8)

I believe he tolerates Shylock, neither liking nor loathing him personally, just in the endemic anti-Semitic way of his time and class – it is Shylock who despises Antonio's trade (note the use of the word "squandered"):

> Yet his means are in supposition. He hath an argosy bound
> to Tripolis, another to the Indies; I understand, moreover,
> upon the Rialto, he hath a third at Mexico, a fourth for
> England, and other ventures he hath squandered abroad.
> But ships are but boards, sailors but men; there be land rats
> and water rats, water thieves and land thieves, I mean
> pirates; and then there is the peril of waters, winds and
> rocks.
>
> (Act I, scene 3, 17-24)

and actively detests Antonio himself:

> I hate him for he is a Christian;
> But more, for that in low simplicity
> He lends out money gratis and brings down
> The rate of usance here with us in Venice.
> If I can catch him once upon the hip,
> I will feed fat the ancient grudge I bear him.
> He hates our sacred nation and he rails
> Even there where merchants most do congregate
> On me, my bargains, and my well-won thrift,
> Which he calls interest.
>
> (Act I, scene 3, 39-48)

This is the background to the eventual grudge fight in court later.

So, is the play the story of Antonio? As I will show, his is but one strand in a complex weave – no more or less important than the other strands.

# 2

# Lorenzo and Bassanio

It is a cheap, but nevertheless informative, trick to divide the cast of any play into the characters you like, the ones you should like (but perhaps don't) and those you don't like. I am firmly of the view that the 'nice guys' in *The Merchant of Venice* are Lorenzo, Gratiano (if, and only if, you can forgive him his hysterical outbursts at the trial!), Nerissa and Launcelot.

Lorenzo is all heart. He is the romantic headstrong fool personified. He is rash, no doubt handsome, and astonishingly wise over matters of harmony and grace. Indeed, Shakespeare gives him some of the best and most beautiful verse in the entire play:

> How sweet the moonlight sleeps upon this bank!
> Here will we sit and let the sounds of music
> Creep in our ears; soft stillness and the night
> Become the touches of sweet harmony.
> Sit, Jessica. Look how the floor of heaven
> Is thick inlaid with patens of bright gold.
> There's not the smallest orb which thou beholdest
> But in his motion like an angel sings,
> Still quiring to the young-eyed cherubins;
> Such harmony is in immortal souls,
> But whilst this muddy vesture of decay
> Doth grossly close it in, we cannot hear it.
> (Act V, scene 1, 54-65)

and:

> The man that hath no music in himself,
> Nor is not moved with concord of sweet sounds,
> Is fit for treasons, stratagems and spoils,
> The motions of his spirit are dull as night,
> And his affections dark as Erebus.
> Let no such man be trusted.
> 
> (Act V, scene 1, 83-8)

But he is foolish in other ways, not least in his rash elopement with Jessica where he seems to have been blinded by lust. He has his eye to the main chance, but it is Jessica who provides the money, not Lorenzo who requests it:

> JESSICA
> I will make fast the doors, and gild myself
> With some more ducats, and be with you straight.
> *Exit above*
> GRATIANO
> Now by my hood, a gentle and no Jew!
> LORENZO
> Beshrew me but I love her heartily!
> For she is wise, if I can judge of her,
> And fair she is, if that mine eyes be true,
> And true she is, as she hath proved herself;
> And therefore, like herself, wise, fair and true,
> Shall she be placèd in my constant soul.
> 
> (Act II, scene 6, 49-57)

It is interesting to compare Bassanio's approach to Portia:

> In Belmont is a lady richly left,
> And she is fair, and, fairer than that word,
> Of wondrous virtues. Sometimes from her eyes
> I did receive fair speechless messages.
> Her name is Portia, nothing undervalued
> To Cato's daughter, Brutus' Portia;
> Nor is the wide world ignorant of her worth,
> For the four winds blow in from every coast
> Renownèd suitors, and her sunny locks

> Hang on her temples like a golden fleece,
> Which makes her seat of Belmont Colchos' strond,
> And many Jasons come in quest of her.
> O my Antonio, had I but the means
> To hold a rival place with one of them,
> I have a mind presages me such thrift
> That I should questionless be fortunate.
>
> (Act I, scene 1, 161-76)

Yes, it is clear that he thinks she is wonderful and she obviously was attracted to him, but you are in no doubt that it is the money that Bassanio is after: why else does the speech start with the reference to her being "richly left" and only later mentions that, oh by the way, she is fair? The whole point of the expedition, at least at the start, is to win money to repay Antonio not only the latest stake (the first arrow) but also pay all the previous debts, with interest (the second arrow).

> In my schooldays, when I had lost one shaft,
> I shot his fellow of the self-same flight
> The self-same way, with more advisèd watch,
> To find the other forth; and by adventuring both
> I oft found both.
>
> (Act I, scene 1, 140-4)

This is, to me, why Bassanio is such a difficult part for an actor to play. If you have seen the play in several different productions, ask yourself in how many of them did Bassanio come out either memorable or likeable?

It is interesting to ask why Shakespeare contrasts the two young leads in this way. I think that Lorenzo represents the ideal hero who does everything for love and who admires grace and harmony, even though his actions lead to ruin and doubt; while Bassanio represents the real world where motives are tainted and morally dubious, but where good may come out of our best endeavours, even if they are a poor best.

Very recently, Shakespeare had written *Romeo and Juliet*. In that play Romeo is a headstrong fool in love with being in love. Indeed he is scolded for this by Friar Laurence.

> ROMEO
> Thou chidst me oft for loving Rosaline
> FRIAR
> For doting, not for loving, pupil mine.

Through the play he grows in stature and turns from a boy into a man, but it is still his impetuous nature and rash action that finally seal the tragedy. He can be excused because he doesn't receive the letter, but without such impetuosity the lovers would have survived, maybe to live in happiness in banishment. In Lorenzo, Shakespeare is revisiting the same type. Is he reaching the same conclusion? There is no doubt that Lorenzo means well. But he loves Jessica. Now Jessica is the other half of the problem. If Lorenzo had fallen for Nerissa, the outcome may well have been very different. Jessica is a rebellious and scheming girl. No doubt she loves Lorenzo, but she does see him as her way out of the restrictive servitude in which she is kept by her father:

> And, Launcelot, soon at supper shalt thou see
> Lorenzo, who is thy new master's guest.
> Give him this letter; do it secretly.
> And so farewell; I would not have my father
> See me in talk with thee.
> …
> Alack, what heinous sin is it in me
> To be ashamed to be my father's child.
> But though I am a daughter to his blood,
> I am not to his manners. O Lorenzo,
> If thou keep promise, I shall end this strife,
> Become a Christian and thy loving wife.
> (Act II, scene 3, 5-21)

Unscrupulous and headstrong, she steals all Shylock's jewels and cash:

> I will make fast the doors, and gild myself
> With some more ducats, and be with you straight.
> (Act II, scene 6, 49-50)

As I shall discuss later in connection with Shylock, it is this rash act which must be the final tipping point that takes her father over the edge into his mad vendetta:

> TUBAL
> Your daughter spent in Genoa, as I heard, one night fourscore ducats.
>
> SHYLOCK
> Thou stick'st a dagger in me. I shall never see my gold again. Fourscore ducats at a sitting, fourscore ducats!
>
> TUBAL
> There came divers of Antonio's creditors in my company to Venice that swear he cannot choose but break.
>
> SHYLOCK
> I am very glad of it. I'll plague him; I'll torture him. I am glad of it.
>
> TUBAL
> One of them showed me a ring that he had of your daughter for a monkey.
>
> SHYLOCK
> Out upon her! Thou torturest me, Tubal. It was my turquoise; I had it of Leah when I was a bachelor. I would not have given it for a wilderness of monkeys.
> (Act III, scene 1, 98-113)

Thus the headstrong love affair between Lorenzo and Jessica (at least as reported by Tubal, who may very well be a wind-up merchant with his own business-driven agenda) sparks the tragedy of Shylock, as compared with that of Romeo and Juliet which leads to their own tragic end. In either affair the end is disaster. To me, therefore, Lorenzo is both an embodiment of the poetic and romantic sensibility – a true 'hero', unlike Bassanio – but also the unwitting dupe in Jessica's flight from servitude.

Bassanio is a different kind of man altogether. He may change during the course of the play, but when we first meet him there is little doubt that he is a deeply flawed young man. The first intimation of this is the curious coolness and distance between him and Antonio's other friends – even Lorenzo.

SALERIO
    Good morrow, my good lords.
BASSANIO
    Good signors both, when shall we laugh? Say, when?
    You grow exceeding strange. Must it be so?
SALERIO
    We'll make our leisures to attend on yours.
                  *Exeunt Selario and Solanio*
LORENZO
    My Lord Bassanio, since you have found Antonio,
    We two will leave you;
                          (Act I, scene1, 65-70)

As soon as Bassanio appears, all the others, including Lorenzo, choose to depart. Gratiano lingers the departure with a sally of wit and concern, but even he goes because he knows Bassanio wants something. It is quite striking, when played, that Bassanio effectively clears the decks. Antonio knows this and immediately asks him what he wants (this time). Bassanio explains in a speech which is breathtaking in its worldly bluntness:

    'Tis not unknown to you, Antonio,
    How much I have disabled mine estate
    By something showing a more swelling port
    Than my faint means would grant continuance.
    Nor do I now make moan to be abridged
    From such a noble rate; but my chief care
    Is to come fairly off from the great debts
    Wherein my time, something too prodigal,
    Hath left me gaged. To you, Antonio,
    I owe the most in money and in love,
    And from your love I have a warranty
    To unburden all my plots and purposes
    How to get clear of all the debts I owe.
                         (Act I, scene1, 122-34)

So the whole purpose of the request is to pay off debts, not the least to Antonio. How does he plan to do this? Why, by borrowing yet more money from Antonio and risking it on a desperate venture. So far, fair enough, you might say. But what is the venture? Why, nothing less than a hunting expedition to win the hand of a rich heiress that Bassanio knows has fallen in love with him. He sums it up in the beautiful, but callous, speech quoted above:

> In Belmont is a lady richly left ...
> (Act I, scene 1, 161)

Antonio then does exactly what Bassanio knows he will do – he lends him the money. But Antonio does not have the money and must borrow it. In doing so he unheedingly puts himself into the hands of Shylock.

It is one of the structural devices of the play that nearly all the main action involves a character hazarding something. Bassanio hazards his friend's money to finance his latter day quest for the golden fleece. Antonio out of his love for Bassanio hazards his life to finance the scheme. Launcelot takes a risk in leaving Shylock's employment where the food and pickings are good, to go and work for the spendthrift Bassanio. He is thus able to act as a go-between for Jessica and Lorenzo. Jessica risks ruin and rejection by her father in eloping with Lorenzo. And of course Portia takes an enormous risk in going to the court in Venice in disguise. Even the cool and sensible Gratiano and Nerissa gamble their marriage on Bassanio succeeding in his quest.

Bassanio's second gamble is in choosing a casket and it is here I think that we first begin to see the spoilt boy start to become a man.

Up until this point we see Bassanio as a money-grubbing pampered brat despised by Antonio's other friends. True, he talks of love to Portia in the prelude to the third Casket scene:

> BASSANIO
>                 Let me choose,
>   For as I am, I live upon the rack.
> PORTIA
>   Upon the rack, Bassanio? Then confess
>   What treason there is mingled with your love.
> BASSANIO
>   None but that ugly treason of mistrust
>   Which makes me fear th' enjoying of my love.

> There may as well be amity and life
> 'Tween snow and fire, as treason and my love.

But even Portia, who is clearly besotted with him sounds a note of caution:

> Ay, but I fear you speak upon the rack,
> Where men enforcèd do speak anything.

An interesting dramatic crux comes in his reply to this – do we believe him?

> BASSANIO
> Promise me life and I'll confess the truth.
> PORTIA
> Well then, confess and live.
> BASSANIO
> Confess and love
> Had been the very sum of my confession.
> O happy torment, when my torturer
> Doth teach me answers for deliverance.
> (Act III, scene 2, 24-38)

I think you must believe him. If you cannot, then Portia's stature as a wise heroine is undermined and, for it to be a comedy and not a tragedy, you have to believe that theirs will be a happy marriage. Whether it truly will be is one of the intriguing ambiguities of the play. Does Bassanio really love Portia? Does he really love Antonio? Does he love both? Or, more worryingly, does he perhaps love neither? The director and the actor must at least ask the questions.

The 'hero' status of Bassanio is further advanced in his sober and thoughtful approach to the casket riddles. This, I think, is where the Princes of Morocco and Arragon are more than just precursors in a three-part tale. Morocco is a caricature of the 'hero', a fierce brave warrior who is deeply in love – with himself. When confronted with the caskets, his approach is to be swayed by the outward show, the feeling that anything of true worth must be richly presented.

Arragon, on the other hand, is a figure of fun – an extended anti-Spanish joke which would have been topically hilarious to a 16th-century London audience. He is vain and shallow, arrogant (as his name punningly implies) and foolish. He assumes that he deserves the lady but, as the casket accurately foretells, he gets exactly what he deserves – a fool's head.

In contrast – and clearly Shakespeare intends the comparison, even if at a subliminal level – Bassanio is noble and wise. His analysis of the competing claims of the caskets is a marvel of cool, possibly slightly cynical, wisdom and maturity. Take, for instance:

> Look on beauty,
> And you shall see 'tis purchased by the weight,
> Which therein works a miracle in nature,
> Making them lightest that wear most of it.
> So are those crispèd snaky golden locks,
> Which make such wanton gambols with the wind
> Upon supposèd fairness, often known
> To be the dowry of a second head,
> The skull that bred them in the sepulchre.
> (Act III, scene 2, 88-96)

This, you feel, is a boy who knows the world. Here is proof that the spoilt, indulged brat might perhaps have learnt something in his mercenary dealings. His dismissal of the silver casket is equally telling:

> Therefore, thou gaudy gold,
> Hard food for Midas, I will none of thee;
> Nor none of thee, thou pale and common drudge
> 'Tween man and man

Instead (hurrah!) he chooses the leaden casket:

> But thou, thou meagre lead
> Which rather threaten'st than dost promise aught,
> Thy paleness moves me more than eloquence,
> And here choose I. Joy be the consequence!
> (Act III, scene 2, 101-7)

and in this moment we see Bassanio begin to grow into a hero we can warm to and accept.

The actor's problem is that (as is often the case in Shakespeare) he is given very little lead-in to the change. It is why Bassanio is such a difficult character to bring off. However, at the end of the scene he is given the chance to show us his new-found (at least by us) sensitivity and nobility when presented with Antonio's letter by the fleeing Lorenzo. The enormity of what he has unthinkingly done to the friend who loves him is frankly confessed:

> I freely told you all the wealth I had
> Ran in my veins – I was a gentleman –
> And then I told you true; and yet, dear lady,
> Rating myself at nothing, you shall see
> How much I was a braggart. When I told you
> My state was nothing, I should then have told you
> That I was worse than nothing; for indeed
> I have engaged myself to a dear friend,
> Engaged my friend to his mere enemy
> To feed my means. Here is a letter, lady,
> The paper as the body of my friend,
> And every word in it a gaping wound
> Issuing life-blood.
> (Act III, scene 2, 254-66)

In order to dramatically emphasise his inclusion into the ranks of the good and sympathetic, Shakespeare has him read out loud Antonio's letter. This can be played in various ways, but I found that what worked superbly was for Bassanio to be so overcome during the reading that he can hardly breathe the words of the last sentence without breaking down.

> *Sweet Bassanio, my ships have all miscarried, my creditors grow cruel, my estate is very low, my bond to the Jew is forfeit. And since in paying it, it is impossible I should live, all debts are cleared between you and I if I might but see you at my death. Notwithstanding, use your pleasure. If your love do not persuade you to come, let not my letter.*
> (Act III, scene 2, 315-21)

Bassanio is by now well on the way to becoming truly a hero.

The next time we see him is at the trial where he desperately tries to stop Shylock. First he tries reasoning with him in an exchange that is positively Wildean in its symmetry:

> BASSANIO
>   This is no answer, thou unfeeling man,
>   To excuse the current of thy cruelty.
> SHYLOCK
>   I am not bound to please thee with my answers.
> BASSANIO
>   Do all men kill the things they do not love?
> SHYLOCK
>   Hates any man the thing he would not kill?
> BASSANIO
>   Every offence is not a hate at first.
> SHYLOCK
>   What, wouldst thou have a serpent sting thee twice?
> ANTONIO
>   I pray you think you question with the Jew.
>   You may as well go stand upon the beach
>   And bid the main flood bate his usual height.

When that fails, as we know it will, he tries bargaining (he does come from a speculating entrepreneurial background after all) :

> BASSANIO
>   For thy three thousand ducats here is six.
> SHYLOCK
>   If every ducat in six thousand ducats
>   Were in six parts, and every part a ducat,
>   I would not draw them. I would have my bond.
>                                   (Act IV, scene 1, 63-87)

And finally he makes an impassioned pledge of his life for Antonio's:

> PORTIA
>   Is he not able to discharge the money?
> BASSANIO
>   Yes, here I tender it for him in the court,
>   Yea, twice the sum. If that will not suffice,
>   I will be bound to pay it ten times o'er
>   On forfeit of my hands, my head, my heart.

> If this will not suffice, it must appear
> That malice bears down truth. And I beseech you,
> Wrest once the law to your authority,
> To do a great right, do a little wrong,
> And curb this cruel devil of his will.
> 
> (Act IV, scene 1, 205-14)

Is this merely a hot-headed futile gesture made by a headstrong young man? Possibly, but I like to think – and indeed, the acceptance of Bassanio as a hero demands it – that it is rather a noble and self-sacrificing offer made by a man who is no longer a boy and who knows the astonishing depth and value of the love he receives from Antonio, not least in Antonio's declaration at what he expects to be his death:

> Say how I loved you, speak me fair in death,
> And when the tale is told, bid her be judge
> Whether Bassanio had not once a love.
> 
> (Act IV, scene 1, 272-4)

Indeed, he goes further:

> Antonio, I am married to a wife
> Which is as dear to me as life itself,
> But life itself, my wife, and all the world
> Are not with me esteemed above thy life.
> I would lose all, ay sacrifice them all
> Here to this devil, to deliver you.

At this point Shakespeare reminds us in a gentle but masterly way that this is, after all, a comedy and that it will come out all right at the end, by having Portia (and in the following lines cleverly mirrored by Nerissa) share with the audience her reaction to this offer!

> PORTIA
> Your wife would give you little thanks for that
> If she were by to hear you make the offer.
> GRATIANO
> I have a wife who I protest I love;

> I would she were in heaven, so she could
> Entreat some power to change this currish Jew.
> NERISSA
> 'Tis well you offer it behind her back,
> The wish would make else an unquiet house.
>
> (Act IV, scene 1, 279-91)

What a marvellous piece of dry understatement that "unquiet house" is! It always gets a laugh which relieves the solemnity of the scene. But you do not doubt the seriousness of Bassanio's intentions (who knows about Gratiano's?).

Underneath, of course, it also raises unresolved thoughts about the relative values of the two loves: for Antonio and for Portia. To my mind it is never fully resolved. This is why I wonder whether the marriage will ever be truly happy, but because it is a comedy you don't look that closely while it is played.

To the end then, Bassanio is a 'difficult' character: an importunate and spoiled boy who matures into a man loved by two people in a way that remains ambiguous.

# 3

# Shylock

The second strand of the play concerns the story of Shylock – an alien in a foreign land who has become successful but who risks his wealth, his place among his friends, and even his life, to revenge.

He is indeed an alien. As Portia states in the trial scene:

> It is enacted in the laws of Venice,
> If it be proved against an alien
> That by direct or indirect attempts
> He seek the life of any citizen,
> The party 'gainst the which he doth contrive
> Shall seize one half his goods, the other half
> Comes to the privy coffer of the state,
> And the offender's life lies in the mercy
> Of the Duke only, 'gainst all other voice
> (Act IV, scene 1, 345-53)

Note the contrast between the (Christian) 'citizen' and the (Jewish) 'alien'. He does not belong; he does not have the rights of a citizen, but he is subject to the laws of the state. How long his family has lived in Venice we do not know. It could have been for generations or they could be immigrants. Certainly on the stage the alien nature is emphasised if he is played as an immigrant, if not necessarily a recent one – it heightens the enmity between him and the businessmen like Antonio. As I pointed out in Chapter 1, it is in fact Shylock who resents Antonio more than the other way round:

> in low simplicity
> He lends out money gratis and brings down
> The rate of usance here with us in Venice.
>
> (Act I, scene 3, 40-2)

The 'us' suggests a reputation in an existing market, not the position of an immediate arrival. In any event, Venice clearly has two opposed trade blocks: the Christian entrepreneurs like Antonio and the Jewish money market. Shakespeare would have known that Venice stood on the threshold of trade with the east and was populated by all sorts, and was not so very different from London.

So the Jews had a huge amount of commercial power. What they lacked was freedom. The laws required that they live in a designated area – the Ghetto. In *Venice and Environs: Jewish Itineraries*, ed. Francesca Brandes, the authors write:

> With the arrival of the so-called *nazione ponentina* (the Sephardic Jews) in 1589, the Venice ghetto took on its definitive form: loan banks and second-hand cloth shops and various synagogues distributed around the main *campo* ... the ghetto became a centre of trade not only for Jewish residents and visitors but also for the Christian Venetians, who poured into the district every morning when the gates were opened.
>
> ... Within the gates of the ghetto there were not only places of worship and study but also a theatre, an academy of music and literary salons. The main *calle* of the Ghetto Vecchio was lined by all sorts of shops from those selling everyday supplies to the booksellers in Campiello delle Scole. There was also a twenty-four-room hotel at the Scuola Levantina, an inn and a hospital.

What is fascinating about this is that the Sephardic Jews had arrived in 1589, only seven or eight years before the play was written.

Of course the term 'ghetto' has gone into the language as the generic term for a place of confinement for a particular race or class. Where Shylock lived was the original. After dark there was a curfew and the Jews should not leave the Ghetto. Whether Shylock gets some form of pass to visit Antonio for dinner, or whether he breaks the law, we do not know.

Apart from the curfew, there were clearly many other restrictions on the Jews in Venice, not the least the ones mentioned by Portia. It is these restrictions, and the perceived narrowness of the traditional life that leads Jessica to escape. Jessica has formed an attachment to Lorenzo – we cannot tell whether as a genuine lover or merely as a bus ticket – and her elopement with a Christian triggers the catastrophe.

Shylock, as we have seen, has a burning dislike of Antonio. Shakespeare gives him motives for this. But when Antonio comes to ask for a loan, I do not believe that *at that time* Shylock intends to kill him. Rather the "merry bond", where Shylock will be entitled to one pound of his flesh if he defaults, is seen as a long-term investment, albeit dressed up as a joke. At that time Shylock cannot *know* that Antonio's ships will fail. He might think it a possibility – but fairly remote. What it does do is deliver Antonio into Shylock's power.

Antonio gets the money and gives it to Bassanio. Bassanio goes off on the hunt for the Golden Fleece, and fate intervenes. Jessica elopes with a Christian, a friend of Antonio. Jessica, Shylock's only child, is the mainstay of his house – indeed his only relative as far as we know, his wife Leah having died. Not only does she elope, but she steals all his money and jewels. Where before he merely despised Antonio, now he hates him and his set with a passion, and he regards his daughter as dead. If only he could strike at him now.

Reports come in of Antonio's ruin and the profligate life being led by Jessica and Lorenzo. Not least the report from his 'friend' Tubal.

Ah, Tubal! The little scene with Tubal (Act III, scene 1) is one of the major turning points in the play. It is a masterpiece of subtle manipulation. What does Tubal stand to gain – apart from malicious pleasure – *schadenfreude* – in Shylock's distress? We do not know. We can reflect that it is not honest, whether intentionally or not. The facts are wrong: not all the ships are lost; and we simply do not know if the turquoise was indeed swapped for a monkey. I do not believe Lorenzo would do that. (Interestingly, at the end of the Radford film, Jessica is seen with a jewel of that description). But that goad is the final push that Shylock needs to seek revenge and so to bring about his own ruin. He snaps. From then on he is intent only on Antonio's downfall, unwittingly bringing on his own instead. This is the true tragedy at the heart of this 'comedy'.

He has Antonio arrested and thrown in prison. He gives him no mercy. He delights in his discomfiture. He is no longer a sane, rational man. He throws away everything he has on a desperate wager on the bond. The tragedy of a straight (I think honourable) man reduced to becoming a figure of hate is almost unbearable.

It is essential that on the stage Shylock is not presented from the outset as a villain. In previous (anti-Semitic) traditions, he was played as an evil-looking monster from the start. I think Shakespeare would have been appalled. He must appear as a reasonable, if very narrow, honourable man. Even at the start of the trial this must be so. Portia's opening question is

> Which is the merchant here? And which the Jew?
>
> DUKE
> Antonio and old Shylock, both stand forth.
>
> PORTIA
> Is your name Shylock?
>
> SHYLOCK
> Shylock is my name.
>
> PORTIA
> Of a strange nature is the suit you follow,
> Yet in such rule that the Venetian law
> Cannot impugn you as you do proceed.
>
> (Act IV, scene 1, 171-6)

Portia is not being disingenuous. Antonio and Shylock must look similar. This is much easier to achieve if the play is set in a period more recent than the late 16th century. I set the play in the early years of the 20th century, around 1905. At that time big western commercial cities like London and Manchester were thronged with immigrant Jews from Eastern Europe. From the 1880s Jews had fled Russia, Poland and the Baltic States where pogroms (now referred to as ethnic cleansing) had uprooted thousands from their native towns and villages. Many settled in London's East End. In his book *Bloody*

*Foreigners*, Robert Winder describes the effect that the influx had in Britain:

> In 1886, Bismarck expelled 'alien Poles' (i.e. Jews) from Prussia. The Russians responded by banishing Jews from Moscow in 1890. In 1900, some 3,000 Jews left Romania and walked west, crossing Europe by foot until they arrived on British soil. Between 1881 and 1914, some 150,000 Jewish settlers came to Britain ...
>
> Soon there was a virulent chorus of voices raised in protest at the process (1887 was a year of heavy unemployment). The *Evening News* began a campaign against the 'foreign flood', and the Conservative MPs for Bow and Stepney campaigned fiercely against their new constituents, whom they called 'Yids', and managed to create a noisy faction in their party that demanded action ...
>
> The campaign chimed with public opinion and drew supporters from all sectors of society: nationalist Tories and Anglicans, resentful trade unionists, even nervous Jewish grandees and socialist ideologues all found a home in the anti-alien movement ...
>
> Finally, on 10th August 1905, after more than a decade of lobbying and election promises by the Tories, the Conservative government passed the Aliens Act.

The Aliens Act curtailed the liberty of immigrants. Apart from the jolting parallels with today, you will see how setting the play in the first decade of the 20th century provides a highly recognisable equivalent of the more remote 16th century. Not least, the business men – the Shylocks and the Antonios – would dress similarly, so Portia would realistically be able to ask which was which in Court. The above passage also, I am sure, parallels the kind of hostility that would have been present in Venice.

It was certainly present in London. In 1593, Rodrigo Lopez, a Jewish-Portuguese doctor, who had come to England and set up as a doctor in London, having fled persecution by the Inquisition in Portugal, succeeded in his adopted country and became house physician at St Bartholomew's Hospital. In spite of professional jealousy and racial prejudice, he had gathered a distinguished clientele and in 1586 he scaled the peak of his profession when he was made physician-in-chief to Queen Elizabeth herself. Vicious rumours were spread that he owed his advancement less to his medical knowledge than to "flattery and self-advertisement" and a libellous pamphlet insinuated that he had served Leicester all too well – by distilling poisons for him. But Dr Lopez was safe in the Queen's protection and could not be touched. So, by 1593 he was a practising Christian, with all the fruits of success, including a son at Winchester School and a house in fashionable Holborn.

In 1594, a plot against the Crown was exposed and Dr Lopez was falsely implicated, in an obsessively anti-Spanish attack by the Earl of Essex. Even though the Queen had herself poured scorn on the attack by Essex, declaring that he was "a rash and temerarious youth, to enter into the matter against the poor man, which he could not prove, but whose innocence she knew well enough". Further evidence against him was obtained using torture and Essex was able to crow that "I have discovered a most dangerous and desperate treason. The point of conspiracy was her Majesty's death. The executioner should have been Dr Lopez; the manner poison. This I have so followed as I will make it appear clear as noon day". Lopez went to trial in February 1594, was found guilty, having "judgment ... passed against him, with the applause of all the world".

Famously, the Queen still could not accept his guilt and refused to sign the death warrant for three months. Nevertheless, on 7th June 1594, only two or three years before *The Merchant of Venice* was written, he was finally executed in the then traditional way for traitors: hanged, drawn, and quartered in front of a baying mob.

This is the background against which Shakespeare wrote the Shylock story. It is easy to see echoes in the jeering calls by Gratiano at the trial. To me, however, Shakespeare has a great deal of sympathy for his tragic protagonist and clearly thought little of Essex and his claque.

Shylock though, is an outsider, principally. Historically, it should be remembered that Jews were not formally admitted into England until years after Shakespeare's death – in Cromwell's time.

Shylock is always presented to us neutrally and without 'spin'. A picture emerges of a punctilious, rather rigid, man. He trusts his daughter with his 'sober' house and valuables although he is insistent about their keep:

> What, are there masques? Hear you me, Jessica:
> Lock up my doors; and when you hear the drum
> And the vile squealing of the wry-necked fife,
> Clamber not you up to the casements then,
> Nor thrust your head into the public street
> To gaze on Christian fools with varnished faces;
> But stop my house's ears, I mean my casements;
> Let not the sound of shallow foppery enter
> My sober house.
>
> (Act II, scene 5, 27-35)

His trust is, of course, betrayed by Jessica.

He enters a commercial deal with the hated Antonio but he is polite even when railed at by him:

> Shall I bend low, and in a bondman's key,
> With bated breath and whispering humbleness,
> Say this:
> 'Fair sir, you spat on me on Wednesday last,
> You spurned me such a day, another time
> You called me dog, and for these courtesies
> I'll lend you thus much moneys'?
> ANTONIO
> I am as like to call thee so again,
> To spit on thee again, to spurn thee too.
> If thou wilt lend this money, lend it not
> As to thy friends, for when did friendship take
> A breed for barren metal of his friend?
> But lend it rather to thine enemy,
> Who if he break, thou mayst with better face
> Exact the penalty.
>
> (Act I, scene 3, 120-34)

Is the politeness mere play-acting designed to lure Antonio into his web? I don't think so. I prefer to believe that he really does enter into the bond as a (sour) jest – not as a carefully premeditated plot.

He is courteous to his greedy servant Launcelot Gobbo when he might be curt or dismissive, even though he might be happy to inflict him on Bassanio:

> The patch is kind enough, but a huge feeder,
> Snail-slow in profit, and he sleeps by day
> More than the wildcat. Drones hive not with me;
> Therefore I part with him, and part with him
> To one that I would have him help to waste
> His borrowed purse.
> 
> (Act II, scene 5, 44-9)

In this and similar passages:

> LAUNCELOT
> I beseech you, sir, go. My young master doth expect your reproach.
> SHYLOCK
> So do I his.

there is a sardonic, almost New York, humour that is quite delightful. The man is certainly not a monster.

Of course, he loses his courtesy in the scene where he baits Antonio when he is in the street with the jailer. But by then, as explained above, he has lost all reason. By the trial, he is again very much under control, with the glint of humour still showing:

> Some men there are love not a gaping pig,
> Some that are mad if they behold a cat,
> And others, when the bagpipe sings i' th' nose,
> Cannot contain their urine.
> 
> (Act IV, scene 1, 47-50)

He debates coolly and rationally with Portia on the nature of the law, but is irrationally inflexible in the demands he makes. In the end it is the rigidity, the obsessive attention to the letter of the law that is his undoing when Portia plays him at his own game and refuses him the previously rejected settlement.

> SHYLOCK
> Shall I not have barely my principal?

PORTIA
> Thou shalt have nothing but the forfeiture,
> To be so taken at thy peril, Jew.

SHYLOCK
> Why, then the devil give him good of it!
> I'll stay no longer question.

PORTIA
>                 Tarry, Jew!
> The law hath yet another hold on you.
> It is enacted in the laws of Venice,
> If it be proved against an alien
> That by direct or indirect attempts
> He seek the life of any citizen,
> The party 'gainst the which he doth contrive
> Shall seize one half his goods, the other half
> Comes to the privy coffer of the state,
> And the offender's life lies in the mercy
> Of the Duke only, 'gainst all other voice,
> In which predicament I say thou stand'st
>
>                 (Act IV, scene 1, 339-54)

At the end he is a broken man – I think literally broken: I am sure that the illness is not feigned but real.

SHYLOCK
> I pray you give me leave to go from hence,
> I am not well; send the deed after me,
> And I will sign it.

DUKE
>            Get thee gone, but do it.
>
>                 (Act IV, scene 1, 392-4)

The obvious way to play it is for him to suffer a heart attack or at least a severe bout of angina.

We never see him again, but once he renounces his religion and becomes a Christian all Jewish doors would be shut to him: like his daughter, he would be dead to the society he once knew. Nor would he be accepted (or want to be) by Christian society: one can hardly imagine him down at the tavern with Solanio and that crowd!

His story is a true tragedy in miniature – a proud man brought low by circumstance and his own failings. It is interesting to speculate what the play would have been like if that indeed was the main thrust of the story – the tragedy of Shylock to set alongside the tragedies of Othello, Macbeth or Lear.

# 4

# Portia

Portia is the other 'difficult' character. Who is she? How can we resolve the contrast between the hidebound, dutiful girl of Act I, the brilliant-on-her-feet lawyer of Act IV and the plot-resolving *dea ex machina* of Act V?

When we first meet Portia in Act I, scene 2 she is a light-hearted, giggly girl discussing her suitors with her maid/companion Nerissa. She is established quickly as sharp-witted and wise:

> It is a good divine that follows his own instructions. I can easier teach twenty what were good to be done than to be one of the twenty to follow mine own teaching. The brain may devise laws for the blood, but a hot temper leaps o'er a cold decree.
>
> (Act I, scene 2, 14-18)

There then follow a brilliant series of thumbnail portraits of different characters: the obsessively equestrian Neapolitan prince, the miserable Palatine count, the vain, egotistical French lord, the ignorant English tourist, the brawling Scot, and the German alcoholic. Every one dispatched in a few well-chosen tart phrases – until we come to the Venetian scholar and soldier. Then we sense the already-formed attraction, brushed aside with an embarrassed "Bassanio, as I think, so was he called" which gets a big laugh if the "Bassanio" is heartfelt, wild and enthusiastic, the "as I think …" studiedly and unconvincingly nonchalant.

Already, in this first scene, we get an inkling that the lady is sharper than she looks, but wildly passionate.

In the scenes that follow there is little further development except to underline the fear that one or other of the suitors will succeed and thus prevent her marrying Bassanio. We get a glimpse of her (to modern sensibilities) racist views in her comments on Morocco:

> A gentle riddance. Draw the curtains, go.
> Let all of his complexion choose me so.
> (Act II, scene 7, 77-8)

Depending on the general 'agenda' of a modern production, this passage can either be left – making Portia a less sympathetic character to the modern audience – or the second line of the couplet can be cut. I chose the latter course, but it is a difficult decision to take. There is an undeniable racist strain in Portia that surfaces again as sneering use of the term "Jew" in the trial scene [my italics]:

> PORTIA
>   Thou shalt have nothing but the forfeiture,
>   To be so taken at thy peril, *Jew*.
> SHYLOCK
>   Why, then the devil give him good of it!
>   I'll stay no longer question.
> PORTIA
>                         Tarry, *Jew*!
>   The law hath yet another hold on you.
>                         (Act IV, scene 1, 340-4)

That use cannot but be seen as antagonistic and anti-Semitic. She could use his name: she has earlier specifically been given it by the Duke.

I suspect that this would not have been worth mentioning at the time the play was written – one would expect a lazy, unthinking anti-Semitism (and indeed general jingoism) from the upper classes then – but it does jar now. It is very much Portia's and Gratiano's attitude at the trial that makes people consider the play to be anti-Semitic, not the actions of Antonio or the Duke. The Duke indeed is truly merciful, commuting the sentence:

> That thou shalt see the difference of our spirit,
> I pardon thee thy life before thou ask it.
> For half thy wealth, it is Antonio's,
> The other half comes to the general state,
> Which humbleness may drive unto a fine.
>
> (Act IV, scene 1, 365-9)

Portia is thus clearly described as an intelligent, witty, unthinking racist, not afraid of showing off in her disguise. She is deeply in love with Bassanio, now her very recent husband, but cannot accede to his impassioned requests in the Court.

> PORTIA
> Is he not able to discharge the money?
> BASSANIO
> Yes, here I tender it for him in the court,
> Yea, twice the sum. If that will not suffice,
> I will be bound to pay it ten times o'er
> On forfeit of my hands, my head, my heart.
> If this will not suffice, it must appear
> That malice bears down truth. And I beseech you,
> Wrest once the law to your authority,
> To do a great right, do a little wrong,
> And curb this cruel devil of his will.
> PORTIA
> It must not be. There is no power in Venice
> Can alter a decree establishèd.
> 'Twill be recorded for a precedent,
> And many an error by the same example
> Will rush into the state. It cannot be.
>
> (Act IV, scene 1, 205-19)

In her disguise, she cannot help hearing Bassanio's declaration that his own life and that of his wife were of less value than the life of his great love Antonio. In the trial scene itself, as mentioned earlier, this is passed off with a sharp witticism, but you are left wondering whether she might not have some doubts about the basis on which her marriage rests! This, I think, is what gives the subsequent ring plot its deep psychological undertow.

When Bassanio asks whether he can pay the clever young doctor,

Portia first asks for a glove in a kind of mirror image of a challenge to a duel and then she sees her ring on his finger. Seeing in an instant a way to truly challenge him and test whether his love for her is stronger than his love for Antonio, she demands the ring as her fee. To his credit and to her satisfaction, he withstands the test and refuses to part with the ring.

Who changes his mind? – Antonio.

> ANTONIO
> My Lord Bassanio, let him have the ring.
> Let his deservings, and my love withal,
> Be valued 'gainst your wife's commandèment.
> (Act IV, scene 1, 446-8)

Note "and my love withal". Antonio is precisely arguing that the love between them is more powerful than Portia's command.

After only a moment's hesitation Bassanio accedes to Antonio's request even though he would not grant the doctor's. And so Gratiano is sent to deliver the ring to Portia. So far, so deeply dubious! But it is a comedy – and so Shakespeare draws back and wraps the bitter pill in a frothy sub-plot involving Gratiano and Nerissa. Comedy it may be, but Portia cannot but be worried.

The next time we see Portia, she is returning from Venice in the dark (in more than one sense!) to a deeply romantic love scene involving Lorenzo and Jessica. There they lie, asleep under the stars, lulled to sleep by sweet harmony. Portia's reaction is interesting:

> Peace!
> How the moon sleeps with Endymion,
> And would not be awaked.
> (Act V, scene 1, 109-10)

The Victorian, Thomas Bulfinch, describes the myth as follows:

> Endymion was a beautiful youth who fed his flock on
> Mount Latmos. One calm, clear night, Diana, the Moon,
> looked down and saw him sleeping. The cold heart of the
> virgin goddess was warmed by his surpassing beauty, and

she came down to him, kissed him, and watched over him while he slept.

However, Romans associated Diana (the Greek Artemis) with Selene, the goddess of the Moon. But while Diana was chaste, Selene was wild and promiscuous. The less romantic view is that when Selene saw Endymion, she fell violently in love and seduced him. At Selene's request Zeus, her father, agreed to grant any wish. He chose the eternal sleep, and fell asleep, remaining young forever.

One wonders quite what Portia's view is. The point of the story in either version is that Diana watched over him as he slept – she did not sleep with him! Thus there is a gentle implied ribbing of both of them for being asleep at their posts, but perhaps an undertow of jealousy that Jessica can be sure of her man (seduced or not) while she has gnawing doubts.

But the whole tenor of the last act is in the restoring of harmony, as heralded by the discussion of the soothing power of music as quoted in Chapter 2. So it is necessary for the ring plot to be happily resolved. Portia's somewhat melancholic view of the early morning light is interrupted by the arrival of Bassanio with Gratiano and Antonio.

> PORTIA
> This night methinks is but the daylight sick,
> It looks a little paler. 'Tis a day
> Such as the day is when the sun is hid.
> …
> BASSANIO
> We should hold day with the Antipodes
> If you would walk in absence of the sun.
> PORTIA
> Let me give light, but let me not be light,
> For a light wife doth make a heavy husband,
> And never be Bassanio so for me.
> But God sort all! You are welcome home, my lord.
> BASSANIO
> I thank you, madam. Give welcome to my friend.
> This is the man, this is Antonio,
> To whom I am so infinitely bound.

PORTIA
> You should in all sense be much bound to him,
> For, as I hear, he was much bound for you.
> (Act V, scene 1, 124-37)

The doubts still linger – observe the fear that Bassanio might be somehow unsatisfactory as a lover and the play on words "in all sense be much bound to him ..." suggesting a bond that she would rather not exist.

It is necessary to remember that the Elizabethan audience would have recognised and enjoyed the references to rings as lewd double entendres. "Ring" was a slang term for arse – a joke that occurs throughout Shakespeare plays. For example, in *King Henry IV, Part I*, Act III, scene 3, Falstaff links "arras" (a pun or near-homophone for arse) with a ring stolen while he was asleep:

> FALSTAFF
> The other night I fell asleep here behind the arras and
> had my pocket picked. This house is turned bawdy
> house; they pick pockets.
> PRINCE HAL
> What didst thou lose, Jack?
> FALSTAFF
> Wilt thou believe me, Hal? Three or four bonds of
> forty pound a-piece and a seal-ring of my grandfather's.

Gratiano makes the same joke in the last lines of the play:

> Whether till the next night she had rather stay,
> Or go to bed now, being two hours to day.
> But were the day come, I should wish it dark
> That I were couching with the doctor's clerk.
> Well, while I live I'll fear no other thing
> So sore as keeping safe Nerissa's ring.
> (Act V, scene 1, 302-7)

Gordon Williams in *A Dictionary of Sexual Language and Imagery in Shakespearean and Stuart Literature* cites the Rabelasian version of the Hans Carvel story (which is behind Gratiano's joke) that concludes with the husband's finding "his finger in his wife's arse" (p.42).

As if to underline the subliminal references to Bassanio's relationship with Antonio which run through the entire scene, Portia has Antonio give Bassanio the ring:

> PORTIA
>     Then you shall be his surety. Give him this,
>     And bid him keep it better than the other.
> ANTONIO
>     Here, Lord Bassanio. Swear to keep this ring.
> BASSANIO
>     By heaven, it is the same I gave the doctor!
> PORTIA
>     I had it of him. Pardon me, Bassanio.
>     For by this ring the doctor lay with me.
>                                     (Act V, scene 1, 254-9)

To a modern audience, these considerations might seem like over-elaboration (and they hardly appear instantaneously during the actual performance of the lines), but the strands are there in the pattern and, acting subliminally, add to the richness and complexity of what is, on the surface, a simple tying-up of ends in the dènouement of a comedy. You sense that Portia in some measure knows that her husband's love will always be divided.

The ending is harmonious, but there is a minor key undertow to the resolving chord: this marriage may only be happy on the surface.

# 5

# Gratiano and Nerissa

At the start, I contrasted Bassanio with Gratiano and Portia with Nerissa. I should now like to develop those comparisons.

Gratiano is a complex character who mysteriously remains likeable even when he is behaving badly. The character seems at first like a worldly-wise, cynical, witty friend. He certainly knows the way of the world:

> There are a sort of men whose visages
> Do cream and mantle like a standing pond,
> And do a wilful stillness entertain
> With purpose to be dressed in an opinion
> Of wisdom, gravity, profound conceit,
> As who should say 'I am Sir Oracle,
> And when I ope my lips, let no dog bark.'
> (Act I, scene 1, 88-94)

Shakespeare uses the device of offsetting the hero with a sharper, funny parallel in other plays written around this time. One thinks particularly of Mercutio in *Romeo and Juliet*:

> ROMEO
>     I dreamt a dream tonight.
> MERCUTIO
>     And so did I.
> ROMEO
>     Well, what was yours?

**MERCUTIO**
>That dreamers often lie.
>>(Act I, scene 4)

Gratiano teases Lorenzo all the time. In the first scene, he even teases the solemn Antonio:

**GRATIANO**
>You look not well, Signior Antonio.
>You have too much respect upon the world;
>They lose it that do buy it with much care.
>Believe me, you are marvellously changed.

**ANTONIO**
>I hold the world but as the world, Gratiano,
>A stage where every man must play a part,
>And mine a sad one.

**GRATIANO**
>>Let me play the fool;
>With mirth and laughter let old wrinkles come,
>And let my liver rather heat with wine
>Than my heart cool with mortifying groans.
>>(Act I, scene 1, 73-82)

but Bassanio dismisses his words:

**BASSANIO**
>Gratiano speaks an infinite deal of nothing, more than any man in all Venice. His reasons are as two grains of wheat hid in two bushels of chaff: you shall seek all day ere you find them, and when you have them they are not worth the search.
>>(Act I, scene 1, 114-8)

Indeed, you feel that Bassanio merely tolerates him in the way that nobility tolerates clowns in Shakespeare – because they keep their feet on the ground. He is certainly very dubious about taking Gratiano to Belmont:

**GRATIANO**
>I have a suit to you.

BASSANIO
>			You have obtained it.
GRATIANO
> You must not deny me. I must go with you to Belmont.
BASSANIO
> Why then you must. But hear thee, Gratiano:
> Thou art too wild, too rude and bold of voice,
> Parts that become thee happily enough
> And in such eyes as ours appear not faults,
> But where thou art not known, why there they show
> Something too liberal.
>			(Act II, scene 2, 165-72)

That "why then you must" is a lovely example of saying one thing while meaning the opposite: you can hear the 'Doh!' immediately before it.

He is only witty on the surface. Underneath there is a hot-blooded, short-tempered rather dangerous character who is the centre of many of the arguably anti-Semitic exchanges in the play, as exemplified neatly by his reaction to Jessica:

JESSICA
> I will make fast the doors, and gild myself
> With some more ducats, and be with you straight.
GRATIANO
> Now by my hood, a gentle and no Jew!
>			(Act II, scene 6, 49-51)

This single line is fraught with double entendre and innuendo. "By my hood" is explained by the editor of the Penguin Shakespeare edition as "an oath by his masque habit, or, ironically, by a monk's hood". These are no doubt true, but a hood, to the coarser part of the audience would surely refer to the foreskin (which of course gentiles have but Jews do not!). Gentle puns with gentile, so Gratiano is claiming Jessica as a gentile with the implicit value judgement that this is better. Lorenzo, of course, sees nothing but good:

LORENZO
> Beshrew me but I love her heartily!
> For she is wise, if I can judge of her,

> And fair she is, if that mine eyes be true,
> And true she is, as she hath proved herself;
> And therefore, like herself, wise, fair and true,
> Shall she be placèd in my constant soul.
>
> (Act II, scene 6, 52-7)

The next time we see Gratiano he is in Belmont with Bassanio as he comes to make his choice of the caskets. Time has passed, during which he has fallen in love with Nerissa and agreed that fate of their union should stand on the same choice that Bassanio makes. This seems wildly improbable, unless Gratiano had seen Nerissa earlier when Bassanio came first to Belmont. We are not told. Bassanio himself is clearly dubious:

> BASSANIO
> And do you, Gratiano, mean good faith?
> GRATIANO
> Yes, faith, my lord.
>
> (Act III, scene 2, 210-11)

As we come to learn, he has indeed met his match in both senses of the phrase. You wonder quite how much it was a case of Nerissa snaring him.

At the trial the wild boy emerges as a ranting heckler with racist tendencies:

> GRATIANO
> Not on thy sole, but on thy soul, harsh Jew,
> Thou mak'st thy knife keen; but no metal can,
> No, not the hangman's axe, bear half the keenness
> Of thy sharp envy. Can no prayers pierce thee?
> SHYLOCK
> No, none that thou hast wit enough to make.
> GRATIANO
> O be thou damned, inexecrable dog,
> And for thy life let justice be accused!
>
> (Act IV, scene 1, 123-9)

and:

> A Daniel still say I, a second Daniel!
> I thank thee, Jew, for teaching me that word.
>
> (lines 337-8)

and:

> Beg that thou mayst have leave to hang thyself,
> And yet, thy wealth being forfeit to the state,
> Thou hast not left the value of a cord,
> Therefore thou must be hanged at the state's charge.
>
> (lines 361-4)

None of these is overtly racist, but certainly marks Gratiano out as intemperate and prejudiced to modern eyes. And yet, through some mysterious magic of Shakespeare's writing, he remains likable. You may disagree!

In the last act, his outraged quarrel with Nerissa is always funny when played to the (operatic) hilt. He, of course, comes off worse. But Shakespeare gives him the last words of the play, which is a clear indication of where his sympathies lie:

> GRATIANO
>     Let it be so. The first inter'gatory
>     That my Nerissa shall be sworn on is
>     Whether till the next night she had rather stay,
>     Or go to bed now, being two hours to day.
>     But were the day come, I should wish it dark
>     Till I were couching with the doctor's clerk.
>     Well, while I live I'll fear no other thing
>     So sore as keeping safe Nerissa's ring.
>
> (Act V, scene 1, 300-7)

It is remarkable that the very last words are, in fact, a dirty joke. I cannot think of another Shakespeare play where this happens. Compare *Twelfth Night* – Feste's plaintive song; *As You Like It* – Rosalind's epilogue; *The Comedy of Errors* – the sweet union of the twin Dromios; and *A Midsummer Night's Dream* – Puck's epilogue. *The Taming of the Shrew* does have what might be a rueful joke about Bianca, but then again might not be, but *The Merchant of Venice* has a real bawdy reference to a woman's arse. To me this is Shakespeare's way of emphasising that the play is, indeed, a comedy, should you otherwise doubt it. The fact that this was felt to be in need of emphasis shows just how ambivalent the endings to the various stories really are.

Gratiano, then, is a comic seasoning to an essentially non-comic series of stories. The other comic is of course Launcelot Gobbo, of whom more later.

Nerissa is a real heroine for me. She is witty, brave, dominant and steadfast. She is, without doubt, the most likable character in the play and is an interesting foil for Portia. The nearest equivalent in Shakespeare is Celia in *As You Like It* who is a witty foil to Rosalind and, like Nerissa, improbably falls in love late in the play. She is a companion or lady's maid. She is described in the cast list as her waiting-woman, but she is clearly a friend and confidante far beyond a mere servant. The exchange which opens the second scene is one of intellectual equals long in the habit of sparring:

> PORTIA
> By my troth, Nerissa, my little body is aweary of this
> great world.
> NERISSA
> You would be, sweet madam, if your miseries were in
> the same abundance as your good fortunes are; and yet
> for aught I see, they are as sick that surfeit with too
> much as they that starve with nothing. It is no mean
> happiness, therefore, to be seated in the mean;
> superfluity comes sooner by white hairs, but competency
> lives longer.
> PORTIA
> Good sentences, and well pronounced.
> NERISSA
> They would be better if well followed.
> (Act I, scene 2, 1-11)

It is amusing to note that, having asked Portia what she thinks of all the various suitors and received the various replies, she then announces that:

> You need not fear, lady, the having any of these lords. They
> have acquainted me with their determinations, which is
> indeed to return to their home and to trouble you with no
> more suit, unless you may be won by some other sort than
> your father's imposition, depending on the caskets.

She then teases Portia about Bassanio and is clearly established as a witty counterpoint to Portia's more solemn character. She is present in the first two casket scenes, but says little. In the third casket scene she and Gratiano announce their engagement and they include a bawdy exchange as a counterpoint to the more serious romantic coupling of Portia and Bassanio:

> BASSANIO
> Our feast shall be much honoured in your marriage.
> GRATIANO
> We'll play with them, the first boy for a thousand ducats.
> NERISSA
> What, and stake down?
> GRATIANO
> No, we shall ne'er win at that sport, and stake down.
> (Act III, scene 2, 212-17)

stake being both a wager and a shaft (which in the carnal sense would not work if down).

This is a very brief rally though, because immediately we are plunged into the darkness of Antonio's apparent ruin.

From then on Nerissa is an able foil to Portia, first in the flight to Venice for the trial and then in the ring plot. Throughout her scenes, she brings a charm and warmth to the play which would otherwise be rather sombre. An interesting comparison is with *All's Well That Ends Well* which, even with Parolles, lacks the joy and fun that Nerissa and Gratiano bring to *The Merchant of Venice*.

# 6

# Send in the clowns

Because Shakespeare writes clown parts into many of his plays it is clear that he had in the company accomplished actors who could play such parts, and that such parts were very popular. They were no doubt very funny. Whether they were fully written, or whether they were merely themes on which the comic actor could riff, is difficult to say. I think the porter in *Macbeth* is clearly such a role. Rather like a pantomime dame today, the actor was free to ad lib topical comments and stories which would amuse the audience – especially the groundlings over whose heads much of the more intellectually lofty material would fly.

The problem with Shakespeare's clowns today is that they are not funny at all. I defy you to find Touchstone or Feste the slightest bit amusing. I know modern audiences laugh politely, and modern directors are adept at squeezing some humour out of them, but the laughter is always that particular kind of laughter you get when a well-brought-up audience knows something in a classic is supposed to be funny and laughs (a little too loudly) out of duty.

In *The Merchant of Venice* it is Gobbo – or more accurately the Gobbos, *père et fils* – who are the clowns who should make us laugh. Do they? Well, I never have.

Take the first scene. Launcelot debates whether to follow the devil or his conscience. The laughs in this come more from the fact that the actor has to use three different voices – his own, the fiend's and his conscience's. A good comic can sometimes work this, but you laugh at him, not at the script.

Then his father arrives on the scene. His father is old and blind. Launcelot decides to pretend that he is a stranger and gives him nonsense directions to Shylock's house. How we all laugh. Then, in one of the cruellest so-called funny scenes in Shakespeare, Launcelot pretends that the old man's son, Launcelot, is dead. The old man is distraught. Did anyone ever find this funny? After they have resolved this, Launcelot tells his father that he has left Shylock's service because he is famished – as he describes it in a rare amusing inversion:

> you may tell every finger I have with my ribs
> (Act II, scene 2, 99)

a statement totally at odds with Shylock's own description of him in a later scene:

> Thou shalt not gormandize as thou hast done with me ...
> And sleep, and snore, and rend apparel out ...
> (Act II, scene 5, 3-5)

Who do you believe? It is funnier for Shylock to be right (and in keeping with the more humane reading of his character) and for Launcelot to be fat and lazy.

After that, his role is that of a good-hearted go-between, fond of Jessica and thankfully short of jokes. Does the fondness for Jessica mean that he sees her as a fellow manipulator? Launcelot is quite sharp enough to have got her measure while working in her house. He knows she is a schemer because he takes part in her subterfuge with Lorenzo. He says he is sorry to see her go, but he has already decided to leave himself. They are clearly a pair of fellow travellers and Launcelot develops as a deeper character than his awful clownish start would makes us believe.

This is shown astonishingly in Act III, scene 5. This is the strangest little scene in the whole play. It only has some 86 lines. Clearly it has as its main purpose the provision of a pause in which Portia and Nerissa can change into their court attire. This is not a flippant remark – Shakespeare was nothing if he was not a practical playwright. Without this scene, the ladies would have no time to take off their dresses and put on some form of doctor's gown and breeches.

But it is a strange interlude. As it starts, Launcelot and Jessica are obviously deep in conversation. Indeed, Lorenzo (who knows Launcelot's carnal nature) later states:

> I shall grow jealous of you shortly, Launcelot, if you thus
> get my wife into corners.
>
> (Act III, scene 5, 26-7)

The nature of the debate, however, is not sexual dalliance, housekeeping or the gossip of the marketplace, but redemption theology. There is a short debate on the laying of the sins of the fathers on the children and the saving of wives – compare the first letter of St Paul to the Corinthians, 7.14:

> The unbelieving wife is sanctified by the husband.

Oh, and the price of pork.

This is heady stuff to fill a few minutes while boy actors change their frocks! To add to the high octane mixture, Lorenzo then comes in and accuses Launcelot of making a negro (sic, but the meaning is negress!) pregnant, thus explaining his potential jealousy. The "negro" is previously unheard of, and is never heard of again. I like to think she is Shylock's scullery maid. We don't know, and we are clearly not supposed to care.

Then with a short verbal duel on an extended pun of "cover" meaning a lid of a dish and a hat doffed by a servant, Launcelot departs.

Alan Rosen, reviewing James Bulman's *The Merchant of Venice* in the *Shakespeare in Performance* series (Manchester University Press, 1991) comments:

> Of any role in the play, Launcelot's is the one most profoundly lodged in its historical milieu, and thus also most profoundly resists being translated effortlessly into the superficially similar but fundamentally different language of modern stage production.

In the last few lines we are given Jessica's view of Bassanio, and whether he truly deserves Portia:

> It is very meet
> The Lord Bassanio live an upright life,
> For having such a blessing in his lady,
> He finds the joys of heaven here on earth,
> And if on earth he do not merit it,
> In reason he should never come to heaven.
>
> (lines 68-73)

Does Jessica know something we don't? It is interesting to have a little reminder of our doubts about him at this stage of the play.

The reason I have spent time in discussing this little scene is that Launcelot is not appearing as a clown – or even as a wise fool in the Feste mould – but as a serious (but not solemn) commentator on serious matters. Why Shakespeare did this, I have no idea, but it rarely seems to be commented on. I can only suggest that he simply got tired of the unfunny material that he was providing the actor (probably Will Kempe) and wrote something that they both thought more interesting. It is indeed interesting material, but is quite ill-served by the position and brevity of the scene.

# 7

# The play on stage

I should like, here, to consider some of the practical problems that arise in staging the play for an English-speaking audience in the 21st century.

The necessity always with Shakespeare is to play it in a way that clearly identifies, to a modern audience with limited knowledge of the Elizabethan society, the social and emotional connections and disconnections between the characters. Human nature never changes. That is why we still respond at a deep personal and atavistic level to the plays of Aeschylus, Sophocles and Seneca, to Noh plays and the Mahabharata. However, societies change and diverge and it is often difficult at a distance (whether temporal or spatial) to interpret the interplay of relationships.

This is, I think, the driving reason for performing the plays of Shakespeare in modern (i.e. contemporary) dress. This is not a recent trend. Indeed, it is certain that Shakespeare's plays were played in contemporary clothes when they were first performed. In the case of the plays set in antique or Roman times, a gesture was made to costume in that the nobility would wear Elizabethan court clothes draped with a suggestion of a toga. Peasants always wore ordinary everyday clothes. References to contemporary clothing occur throughout the classical plays of Shakespeare, the most famous example perhaps being Cleopatra asking for her laces to be cut.

Painting and sculpture have frequently portrayed Shakespearean characters in contemporary dress. Tiepolo's *Antony and Cleopatra* shows them in 17th-century finery (probably of a date earlier than the painting, but certainly not 1st-century!). Eighteenth-century productions in England frequently used modern dress. Johann Zoffany's painting of David Garrick and Mrs Pritchard in *Macbeth* from 1768, shows them in high Georgian, rather than Elizabethan court dress, let alone medieval Scottish clothes.

In order to demonstrate the relationships between the characters in the society of the play, there is often a particular period of more recent history to which the director and designer can refer. *The Merchant of Venice* has been set in the mercantile money-grabbing City of London in the Thatcher years, and more than once in the 1930s. The Thacker/Keegan production for The Royal Shakespeare Company in April 1994 was described by Benedict Nightingale in *The Times* as follows:

> The tubular, multi-level office that fills half the stage is packed with people tapping at computers, making phone calls, and bustling urgently about. It is a place where aggrieved money-men are more likely to stab each other in the back with metaphoric knives rather than slice bits off one another with real ones; but we are used to making such leaps of imagination with RSC productions these days.

I did not see that production, but the sense of menacing, cut-throat capitalism was, apparently, palpable.

Setting the play in the 1930s has the obvious draw that the pitting of established society against the outsider Jew is starkly underlined. To my taste it is a little too obvious, but it serves its purpose well.

Another popular period to choose is the very late 19th century. As I explained in Chapter 4, this was a period of mass migration of Jews from Russia, the Baltic States and Eastern Europe. The period is very well recognised by modern audiences, either from family memories or, second hand, from the films of Merchant-Ivory, from Galsworthy on television, from Mary Poppins, or from the plays of Shaw, Chekov and Ibsen. People immediately understand the social levels, they recognise the clothes. They know what they ate! In comparison, Elizabethan England is a strange, remote place with odd clothes and language and most peculiar food.

In the 1960s, Laurence Olivier played Shylock as a socially inferior, late-Victorian Jewish money man, desperate to fit in to a society that unthinkingly excluded him. I chose the same period and found that the resentment of the too-successful outsider in the cosy money market fitted beautifully into a time when the influx of Jews was causing upheavals in politics and trade in England. I should add that this is very much an English, and probably Irish and American, view of that period. It is worth noting that, at the time we are discussing, Venice itself had a Jewish mayor. I am fairly sure that he would not have been a recent arrival, but the descendant of a prototype for the Shylock of Shakespeare.

Another advantage of the period around the 1890s and 1900 is that it coincides with the Oscar Wilde trials and a flowering of a homosexual aesthetic with *The Yellow Book* and the Bloomsbury set. The relationship of Antonio with Bassanio is entirely credible in the Edwardian clubby atmosphere of that time. Yet another advantage of this time, as compared with modern settings, is that women were still not enfranchised and were under the control of a still very masculine law. The requirements of Portia's late father's will concerning the choosing by casket, is still just about credible at that time, whereas it makes absolutely no sense in the latter half of the 20th century, let alone the 21st.

A practical problem raised in the staging of the play is that in the first three acts, the scene see-saws frequently between Venice and Belmont. Both locations are important and different and it simply will not do to use an all-purpose bare stage approach: you need to be able to see the inter-cutting between the two. On relatively simple stages, this is often achieved by making one side of the stage Venice and the other Belmont and to alter the mood with lighting changes. I adopted this approach with Venice suggested by steps and a bridge as if over a canal and a curving back cloth painted with key words dealing with love and money. As the time of year is clearly late winter – early spring (we can guess this from the fact that the Venice carnival is in progress), Venice was lit with cold, watery light, dappling as if reflected off the ever-present dark waters. Individual scenes like the initial conversation with Antonio and the poignant little scene between

Solanio and Salerio in Act II, scene 8, were played in a pool of dim, warm lamplight. Belmont was just elegant furniture and light which was warm and sunny until the arrival of Antonio's letter whereupon the sky dimmed and the light slowly cooled. The last act starts in darkness with only the lamp used by Lorenzo and Jessica with the candle that shines like a good deed in a naughty world. During that act the dawn approaches and the darkness slowly resolves into daylight as the harmony required for the resolution of the play is achieved. Lighting is thus very useful to establish the very different moods between the two places. The trial scene also tests the stagecraft of the production team. If you get it wrong, the emphasis is too much on Antonio or the Duke, whereas the main duel is between Portia and Shylock. The whole process is most peculiar to an audience steeped in the court protocol of England. Portia assumes the role of examining magistrate and prosecution counsel rather than judge. The Duke effectively presides without taking part in any real sense at all. Where do you put the Duke? At the back, and the various protagonists are upstaged; down front and he blocks the audience's sightlines.

I opted for a diagonal approach with Shylock upstage right and Antonio facing him downstage left, with the Duke raised high upstage, left centre. Portia could then stand below the Duke and face both Shylock and Antonio. The body of the court, with Gratiano and various friends and the curious public, was down right (and, of course the audience themselves were down centre). Shylock was provided with a chair on which to collapse at the end. When he says he is not well, I am inclined to believe him – I think he suffers from angina and is having a mild heart attack.

It is generally the custom now to play with one interval. Originally, there would not have been an interval at all – members of the audience came and went as the requirements of their appetites and bladders dictated. Nowadays there is one, or possibly two, short intervals. Because of this there is actually no need at all for Act III, Scene 8 as Portia and Nerissa could have the interval in which to change. Indeed, the play breaks conveniently at the end of scene 7 with the girls going off to Venice. Omitting Scene 8 solves all the problems raised previously, and is a course frequently taken by modern directors.

The remaining question is how to end the play. At The Globe Theatre in London, the historically conventional ending to a comedy is often used: the entire company join in a celebration dance. Other productions (the Radford film referred to earlier) tend to want to linger on the underlying sadness or unresolved aspect of some of the couplings. It is very tempting to revisit Shylock in his new status as a 'Christian' pariah, unwelcome among the Christians and dead to his Jewish friends. Other productions (mine included) have finished with a last look at Jessica – rich, married, but irrevocably estranged from her father and her roots. Is she happy? Another option is to fade out on Portia and Bassanio and Antonio: is this triangle broken? Has she really got her man?

It is very tempting (and many are so tempted) to shuffle some of the lines of Act V to end on a wistful, rather than a bawdy note. I succumbed to this temptation (and I apologise now to any purists still reading this book at this point) and used the following ending. None of the lines is added: merely rearranged. I maintain it makes a powerfully moving finish and proved so when played:

> NERISSA
>   And pardon me, my gentle Gratiano;
>   For that same scrubbed boy, the doctor's clerk,
>   In lieu of this last night did lie with me.
> GRATIANO
>   Why, this is like the mending of highways
>   In summer, where the ways are fair enough:
>   What, are we cuckolds ere we have deserved it?
> PORTIA
>   Speak not so grossly. You are all amazed.
>   Here is a letter, read it at your leisure.
>   It comes from Padua from Bellario.
>   There you shall find that Portia was the doctor,
>   Nerissa there her clerk. Lorenzo here
>   Shall witness I set forth as soon as you,
>   And even but now returned, I have not yet
>   Entered my house. Antonio, you are welcome,
>   And I have better news in store for you
>   Than you expect. Unseal this letter soon,

    There you shall find three of your argosies
    Are richly come to harbour.
ANTONIO
    I am dumb!
BASSANIO
    Were you the doctor and I knew you not?
GRATIANO
    Were you the clerk that is to make me cuckold?
NERISSA
    Ay, but the clerk that never means to do it,
    Unless he live until he be a man.
BASSANIO
    Sweet doctor, you shall be my bedfellow.
    When I am absent, then lie with my wife.
GRATIANO
    Were the day come, I yet would wish it dark,
    Till I were couching with the doctor's clerk.
    Well, while I live I'll fear no other thing
    So sore as keeping safe Nerissa's ring!
ANTONIO
    Sweet lady, you have given me life and living,
    For here I read for certain that my ships
    Are safely come to road.
PORTIA
                      How now, Lorenzo?
    My clerk hath some good comforts too for you.
NERISSA
    Ay, and I'll give them him without a fee.
    There do I give to you and Jessica
    From the rich Jew, a special deed of gift,
    After his death, of all he dies possessed of.
LORENZO
    Fair ladies, you drop manna in the way
    Of starvèd people.
PORTIA
                      It is almost morning,
    This night methinks is but the daylight sick;
    It looks a little paler: 'tis a day
    Such as the day is when the sun is hid.
BASSANIO
    We should hold day with the antipodes,
    If you walk in absence of the sun.

PORTIA
>Let me give light, but let me be not light;
>For a light wife doth make a heavy husband,
>And never be Bassanio so for me!
>Let us go in.

*Exeunt leaving Jessica behind. In the background Shylock appears with a priest. They both pause. The sound of Jessica singing Kadish is heard faintly.*
*Fade to them and then to black.*

# Bibliography

All play references are from the *Penguin Shakespeare* series: *The Merchant of Venice*, ed. W. Moelwyn Merchant, (Penguin Books, revised edition 2005).

Brandes, Francesca, ed. *Venice and Environs, Jewish Itineraries: Places, History and Art* (Veneto Marsilio, 1997).
*The Guardian*, Friday 3rd September 2004.
Kingston, Jeremy. *The Times*, circa 9th December 1988.
Nightingale, Benedict. *The Times*, 12th April 1994.
Rosen, Alan. 'Impertinent Matters: Lancelot Gobbo and the Fortunes of Performance Criticism', *Connotations* 8.2 (1998/99): http://www.uni-tuebingen.de/uni/nec/rosen82.htm
Williams, Gordon. *A Dictionary of Sexual Language and Imagery in Shakespearean and Stuart Literature*, 3 vols. (London and New Jersey, Athlone P, 1994).
Winder, Robert. *Bloody Foreigners* (Abacus, 2005).

http://www.globalgayz.com/stratford-on-avon.html
http://www.online-literature.com/bulfinch/mythology_fable

# GREENWICH EXCHANGE BOOKS

# STUDENT GUIDE LITERARY SERIES

The Greenwich Exchange Student Guide Literary Series is a collection of critical essays of major or contemporary serious writers in English and selected European languages. The series is for the student, the teacher and 'common readers' and is an ideal resource for libraries. The *Times Educational Supplement* praised these books, saying, "The style of [this series] has a pressure of meaning behind it. Readers should learn from that ... If art is about selection, perception and taste, then this is it."

(ISBN prefix 978-1-871551-   applies)
All books are paperbacks unless otherwise stated

The series includes:
**W.H. Auden** by Stephen Wade (36-5)
**Honoré de Balzac** by Wendy Mercer (48-8)
**William Blake** by Peter Davies (27-3)
**The Brontës** by Peter Davies (24-2)
**Robert Browning** by John Lucas (59-4)
**Lord Byron** by Andrew Keanie (83-9)
**Samuel Taylor Coleridge** by Andrew Keanie (64-8)
**Joseph Conrad** by Martin Seymour-Smith (18-1)
**William Cowper** by Michael Thorn (25-9)
**Charles Dickens** by Robert Giddings (26-9)
**Emily Dickinson** by Marnie Pomeroy (68-6)
**John Donne** by Sean Haldane (23-5)
**Ford Madox Ford** by Anthony Fowles (63-1)
**The Stagecraft of Brian Friel** by David Grant (74-7)
**Robert Frost** by Warren Hope (70-9)
**Thomas Hardy** by Sean Haldane (33-4)
**Seamus Heaney** by Warren Hope (37-2)
**Joseph Heller** by Anthony Fowles (84-6)
**Gerard Manley Hopkins** by Sean Sheehan (77-3)
**James Joyce** by Michael Murphy (73-0)
**Philip Larkin** by Warren Hope (35-8)
**Laughter in the Dark – The Plays of Joe Orton** by Arthur Burke (56-3)
**Sylvia Plath** by Marnie Pomeroy (88-4)
**Poets of the First World War** by John Greening (79-2)
**Philip Roth** by Paul McDonald (72-3)

**Shakespeare's *A Midsummer Night's Dream*** by Matt Simpson (90-7)
**Shakespeare's *King Lear*** by Peter Davies (95-2)
**Shakespeare's *Macbeth*** by Matt Simpson (69-3)
**Shakespeare's *Othello*** by Matt Simpson (71-6)
**Shakespeare's Second Tetralogy: *Richard II – Henry V*** by John Lucas (97-6)
**Shakespeare's *The Merchant of Venice*** by Alan Ablewhite (96-9)
**Shakespeare's *The Tempest*** by Matt Simpson (75-4)
**Shakespeare's *Twelfth Night*** by Matt Simpson (86-0)
**Shakespeare's *The Winter's Tale*** by John Lucas (80-3)
**Shakespeare's Non-Dramatic Poetry** by Martin Seymour-Smith (22-6)
**Shakespeare's Sonnets** by Martin Seymour-Smith (38-9)
**Tobias Smollett** by Robert Giddings (21-1)
**Dylan Thomas** by Peter Davies (78-5)
**Alfred, Lord Tennyson** by Michael Thorn (20-4)
**William Wordsworth** by Andrew Keanie (57-0)
**W.B. Yeats** by John Greening (34-1)

## LITERATURE & BIOGRAPHY

**Matthew Arnold and 'Thyrsis'** *by Patrick Carill Connolly*
Matthew Arnold (1822-1888) was a leading poet, intellect and aesthete of the Victorian epoch. He is now best known for his strictures as a literary and cultural critic, and educationist. After a long period of neglect, his views have come in for a re-evaluation. Arnold's poetry remains less well known, yet his poems and his understanding of poetry, which defied the conventions of his time, were central to his achievement.
The author traces Arnold's intellectual and poetic development, showing how his poetry gathers its meanings from a lifetime's study of European literature and philosophy. Connolly's unique exegesis of 'Thyrsis' draws upon a wide-ranging analysis of the pastoral and its associated myths in both classical and native cultures. This study shows lucidly and in detail how Arnold encouraged the intense reflection of the mind on the subject placed before it, believing in " ... the all importance of the choice of the subject, the necessity of accurate observation; and subordinate character of expression."
Patrick Carill Connolly gained his English degree at Reading University and taught English literature abroad for a number of years before returning to Britain. He is now a civil servant living in London.
**2004 • 180 pages • ISBN 978-1-871551-61-7**

**The Author, the Book and the Reader** *by Robert Giddings*
This collection of essays analyses the effects of changing technology and the attendant commercial pressures on literary styles and subject matter. Authors covered include Charles Dickens, Tobias Smollett, Mark Twain, Dr Johnson and John le Carré.
**1991 • 220 pages • illustrated • ISBN 978-1-871551-01-3**

**Norman Cameron** *by Warren Hope*
Cameron's poetry was admired by Auden; celebrated by Dylan Thomas; valued by Robert Graves. He was described by Martin Seymour-Smith as "one of ... the most rewarding and pure poets of his generation ..." and is at last given a full-length biography. This eminently sociable man, who had periods of darkness and despair, wrote little poetry by comparison with others of his time, but always of a consistently high quality – imaginative and profound.
Warren Hope is a poet, a critic and university lecturer. He lives and works in Philadelphia, where he raised his family.
**2000 • 226 pages • ISBN 978-1-871551-05-1**

**Aleister Crowley and the Cult of Pan** *by Paul Newman*
Few more nightmarish figures stalk English literature than Aleister Crowley (1875-1947), poet, magician, mountaineer and agent provocateur. In this groundbreaking study, Paul Newman dives into the occult mire of Crowley's works and fishes out gems and grotesqueries that are by turns ethereal, sublime, pornographic and horrifying. Like Oscar Wilde before him, Crowley stood in "symbolic relationship to his age" and to contemporaries like Rupert Brooke, G.K. Chesterton and the Portuguese modernist, Fernando Pessoa. An influential exponent of the cult of the Great God Pan, his essentially 'pagan' outlook was shared by major European writers as well as English novelists like E.M. Forster, D.H. Lawrence and Arthur Machen.
Paul Newman lives in Cornwall. Editor of the literary magazine *Abraxas*, he has written over ten books.
**2004 • 222 pages • ISBN 978-1-871551-66-2**

**John Dryden** *by Anthony Fowles*
Of all the poets of the Augustan age, John Dryden was the most worldly. Anthony Fowles traces Dryden's evolution from 'wordsmith' to major poet. This critical study shows a poet of vigour and technical panache whose art was forged in the heat and battle of a turbulent polemical and pamphleteering age. Although Dryden's status as a literary critic has long been established,

Fowles draws attention to his neglected achievements as a translator of poetry. He deals also with the less well-known aspects of Dryden's work – his plays and occasional pieces.

Born in London and educated at the Universities of Oxford and Southern California, Anthony Fowles began his career in film-making before becoming an author of film and television scripts and more than twenty books. Readers will welcome the many contemporary references to novels and film with which Fowles illuminates the life and work of this decisively influential English poetic voice.

**2003 • 292 pages • ISBN 978-1-871551-58-7**

**The Good That We Do** *by John Lucas*

John Lucas' book blends fiction, biography and social history in order to tell the story of his grandfather, Horace Kelly. Headteacher of a succession of elementary schools in impoverished areas of London, 'Hod' Kelly was also a keen cricketer, a devotee of the music hall, and included among his friends the great trade union leader Ernest Bevin. In telling the story of his life, Lucas has provided a fascinating range of insights into the lives of ordinary Londoners from the First World War until the outbreak of the Second World War. Threaded throughout is an account of such people's hunger for education, and of the different ways government, church and educational officialdom ministered to that hunger. *The Good That We Do* is both a study of one man and of a period when England changed, drastically and forever.

John Lucas is Professor Emeritus of the Universities of Loughborough and Nottingham Trent. He is the author of numerous works of a critical and scholarly nature and has published eight collections of poetry.

**2001 • 214 pages • ISBN 978-1-871551-54-9**

**D.H. Lawrence: The Nomadic Years, 1919-1930** *by Philip Callow*

This book provides a fresh insight into Lawrence's art as well as his life. Candid about the relationship between Lawrence and his wife, it shows nevertheless the strength of the bond between them. If no other book persuaded the reader of Lawrence's greatness, this does.

Philip Callow was born in Birmingham and studied engineering and teaching before he turned to writing. He has published 14 novels, several collections of short stories and poems, a volume of autobiography, and biographies on the lives of Chekhov, Cezanne, Robert Louis Stevenson, Walt Whitman and Van Gogh all of which have received critical acclaim. His biography of D.H. Lawrence's early years, *Son and Lover*, was widely praised.

**2006 • 226 pages • ISBN 978-1-871551-82-2**

**Liar! Liar!: Jack Kerouac – Novelist** *by R.J. Ellis*
The fullest study of Jack Kerouac's fiction to date. It is the first book to devote an individual chapter to every one of his novels. *On the Road*, *Visions of Cody* and *The Subterraneans* are reread in-depth, in a new and exciting way. *Visions of Gerard* and *Doctor Sax* are also strikingly reinterpreted, as are other daringly innovative writings, like 'The Railroad Earth' and his "try at a spontaneous *Finnegans Wake*" – *Old Angel Midnight*. Neglected writings, such as *Tristessa* and *Big Sur*, are also analysed, alongside better-known novels such as *Dharma Bums* and *Desolation Angels*.
R.J. Ellis is Senior Lecturer in English at Nottingham Trent University.
**1999 • 294 pages • ISBN 978-1-871551-53-2**

**Musical Offering** *by Yolanthe Leigh*
In a series of vivid sketches, anecdotes and reflections, Yolanthe Leigh tells the story of her growing up in the Poland of the 1930s and the Second World War. These are poignant episodes of a child's first encounters with both the enchantments and the cruelties of the world; and from a later time, stark memories of the brutality of the Nazi invasion, and the hardships of student life in Warsaw under the Occupation. But most of all this is a record of inward development; passages of remarkable intensity and simplicity describe the girl's response to religion, to music, and to her discovery of philosophy.
Yolanthe Leigh was formerly a Lecturer in Philosophy at Reading University.
**2000 • 56 pages • ISBN: 978-1-871551-46-4**

**In Pursuit of Lewis Carroll** *by Raphael Shaberman*
Sherlock Holmes and the author uncover new evidence in their investigations into the mysterious life and writing of Lewis Carroll. They examine published works by Carroll that have been overlooked by previous commentators. A newly-discovered poem, almost certainly by Carroll, is published here.
Amongst many aspects of Carroll's highly complex personality, this book explores his relationship with his parents, numerous child friends, and the formidable Mrs Liddell, mother of the immortal Alice. Raphael Shaberman was a founder member of the Lewis Carroll Society and a teacher of autistic children.
**1994 • 118 pages • illustrated • ISBN 978-1-871551-13-6**

**Poetry in Exile: A study of the poetry of W.H. Auden, Joseph Brodsky & George Szirtes** *by Michael Murphy*
"Michael Murphy discriminates the forms of exile and expatriation with the shrewdness of the cultural historian, the acuity of the literary critic, and

the subtlety of a poet alert to the ways language and poetic form embody the precise contours of experience. His accounts of Auden, Brodsky and Szirtes not only cast much new light on the work of these complex and rewarding poets, but are themselves a pleasure to read." *Stan Smith, Research Professor in Literary Studies, Nottingham Trent University.*

Michael Murphy is a poet and critic. He teaches English literature at Liverpool Hope University College.

**2004 • 266 pages • ISBN 978-1-871551-76-1**

# POETRY

**Adam's Thoughts in Winter** *by Warren Hope*
Warren Hope's poems have appeared from time to time in a number of literary periodicals, pamphlets and anthologies on both sides of the Atlantic. They appeal to lovers of poetry everywhere. His poems are brief, clear, frequently lyrical, characterised by wit, but often distinguished by tenderness. The poems gathered in this first book-length collection counter the brutalising ethos of contemporary life, speaking of, and for, the virtues of modesty, honesty and gentleness in an individual, memorable way.

**2000 • 46 pages • ISBN 978-1-871551-40-2**

**Baudelaire: Les Fleurs du Mal** *Translated by F.W. Leakey*
Selected poems from *Les Fleurs du Mal* are translated with parallel French texts and are designed to be read with pleasure by readers who have no French as well as those who are practised in the French language.

F.W. Leakey was Professor of French in the University of London. As a scholar, critic and teacher he specialised in the work of Baudelaire for 50 years and published a number of books on the poet.

**2001 • 152 pages • ISBN 978-1-871551-10-5**

**'The Last Blackbird' and other poems by Ralph Hodgson** *edited and introduced by John Harding*
Ralph Hodgson (1871-1962) was a poet and illustrator whose most influential and enduring work appeared to great acclaim just prior to, and during, the First World War. His work is imbued with a spiritual passion for the beauty of creation and the mystery of existence. This new selection brings together, for the first time in 40 years, some of the most beautiful and powerful 'hymns to life' in the English language.

John Harding lives in London. He is a freelance writer and teacher and is Ralph Hodgson's biographer.

**2004 • 70 pages • ISBN 978-871551-81-5**

**Lines from the Stone Age** *by Sean Haldane*
Reviewing Sean Haldane's 1992 volume *Desire in Belfast*, Robert Nye wrote in *The Times* that "Haldane can be sure of his place among the English poets." This place is not yet a conspicuous one, mainly because his early volumes appeared in Canada, and because he has earned his living by other means than literature. Despite this, his poems have always had their circle of readers. The 60 previously unpublished poems of *Lines from the Stone Age* – "lines of longing, terror, pride, lust and pain" – may widen this circle.
**2000 • 52 pages • ISBN 978-1-871551-39-6**

**Lipstick** *by Maggie Butt*
*Lipstick* is Maggie Butt's debut collection of poems and marks the entrance of a voice at once questioning and self-assured. She believes that poetry should be the tip of the stiletto which slips between the ribs directly into the heart. The poems of *Lipstick* are often deceptively simple, unafraid of focusing on such traditional themes as time, loss and love through a range of lenses and personae. Maggie Butt is capable of speaking in the voice of an 11th-century stonemason, a Himalayan villager, a 13-year-old anorexic. When writing of such everyday things as nylon sheets, jumble sales, X-rays or ginger beer, she brings to her subjects a dry humour and an acute insight. But beyond the intimate and domestic, her poems cover the world, from Mexico to Russia; they deal with war, with the resilience of women, and, most of all, with love.
Maggie Butt is head of Media and Communication at Middlesex University, London where she has taught Creative Writing since 1990.
**2007 • 72 pages • ISBN 978-1-871551-94-5**

**Martin Seymour-Smith – Collected Poems** *edited by Peter Davies*
To the general public Martin Seymour-Smith (1928-1998) is known as a distinguished literary biographer, notably of Robert Graves, Rudyard Kipling and Thomas Hardy. To such figures as John Dover Wilson, William Empson, Stephen Spender and Anthony Burgess, he was regarded as one of the most independently-minded scholars of his generation, through his pioneering critical edition of Shakespeare's *Sonnets*, and his magisterial *Guide to Modern World Literature*.
To his fellow poets, Graves, James Reeves, C.H. Sisson and Robert Nye – he was first and foremost a poet. As this collection demonstrates, at the centre of the poems is a passionate engagement with Man, his sexuality and his personal relationships.
**2006 • 182 pages • ISBN 978-1-871551-47-1**

**Shakespeare's Sonnets** *by Martin Seymour-Smith*
Martin Seymour-Smith's outstanding achievement lies in the field of literary biography and criticism. In 1963 he produced his comprehensive edition, in the old spelling, of *Shakespeare's Sonnets* (here revised and corrected by himself and Peter Davies in 1998). With its landmark introduction and its brilliant critical commentary on each sonnet, it was praised by William Empson and John Dover Wilson. Stephen Spender said of him "I greatly admire Martin Seymour-Smith for the independence of his views and the great interest of his mind"; and both Robert Graves and Anthony Burgess described him as the leading critic of his time. His exegesis of the *Sonnets* remains unsurpassed.
**2001 • 194 pages • ISBN 978-1-871551-38-9**

**The Rain and the Glass** *by Robert Nye*
When Robert Nye's first poems were published, G.S. Fraser declared in the *Times Literary Supplement*: "Here is a proper poet, though it is hard to see how the larger literary public (greedy for flattery of their own concerns) could be brought to recognize that. But other proper poets – how many of them are left? – will recognize one of themselves."
Since then Nye has become known to a large public for his novels, especially *Falstaff* (1976), winner of the Hawthornden Prize and The Guardian Fiction Prize, and *The Late Mr Shakespeare* (1998). But his true vocation has always been poetry, and it is as a poet that he is best known to his fellow poets. This book contains all the poems Nye has written since his *Collected Poems* of 1995, together with his own selection from that volume. An introduction, telling the story of his poetic beginnings, affirms Nye's unfashionable belief in inspiration, as well as defining that quality of unforced truth which distinguishes the best of his work: "I have spent my life trying to write poems, but the poems gathered here came mostly when I was not."
**2005 • 132 pages • ISBN 978-1-871551-41-9**

**Wilderness** *by Martin Seymour-Smith*
This is Martin Seymour-Smith's first publication of his poetry for more than twenty years. This collection of 36 poems is a fearless account of an inner life of love, frustration, guilt, laughter and the celebration of others. He is best known to the general public as the author of the controversial and bestselling *Hardy* (1994).
**1994 • 52 pages • ISBN 978-1-871551-08-2**

# EDUCATION

**Making School Work** *by Andy Buck*
Full of practical examples, this book sets out a range of strategies for successful school leadership. It provides examples of tried and tested ideas to use when tackling some of the key challenges facing every school leader: This book aims to offer readers a range of practical approaches to both policy and leadership style, based around a series of case studies and school-based policies. Each chapter examines a key challenge facing school leaders and provides practical ideas and strategies that have been shown to work in schools.
A geography teacher since 1987, Andy Bucks' experience has included working as a head of department, head of year, deputy head and two headships, all in London schools.
**2007 • 142 pages • ISBN 978-1-871551-52-5**

# HISTORICAL FACTION

**The Secret Life of Elizabeth I** *by Paul Doherty*
A detective story with a difference – tracking down the real Elizabeth I – capturing the atmosphere of Elizabethan and Jacobean England, with stunning results. Paul Doherty's original research shows Elizabeth I of England to be a strongwilled, brilliant ruler but also a woman with deep passions and fervent attachments. The lady-in-waiting describes the passionate relationship between Elizabeth and Robert Dudley, later Earl of Leicester. She reveals evidence about the strange death of Dudley's wife, the very physical relationship between Elizabeth and Dudley, and the stunning revelation that they had a son, Arthur Dudley, seized by the Spanish in 1587.
Paul Doherty is an internationally renowned author. He studied history at Liverpool and Oxford Universities, gaining his doctorate at Oxford. He is now the headmaster of a very successful London school. First in the series published by Greenwich Exchange.
**2006 • 210 pages • ISBN 978-1-871551-85-3 (Hardback)**

**Death of the Red King** *by Paul Doherty*
Was William Rufus, the Red King, accidentally killed by one of his own men while hunting or is there a more chilling interpretation of his death? Doherty demonstrates that the Red King's death is highly suspect. Walter Tirel has been cast as the villain of the piece. However, through the eyes of Anselm the great philosopher, this faction develops a quite different version

of his death.
Second in the series published by Greenwich Exchange.
**2006 • 190 pages • ISBN 978-1-871551-92-1 (Hardback)**

# BUSINESS

**English Language Skills** *by Vera Hughes*
If you want to be sure, (as a student, or in your business or personal life), that your written English is correct, this book is for you. Vera Hughes' aim is to help you to remember the basic rules of spelling, grammar and punctuation. 'Noun', 'verb', 'subject', 'object' and 'adjective' are the only technical terms used. The book teaches the clear, accurate English required by the business and office world. It coaches acceptable current usage and makes the rules easier to remember.
Vera Hughes was a civil servant and is a trainer and author of training manuals.
**2002 • 142 pages • ISBN 978-1-871551-60-0**